THE FABLES OF LA FONTAINE

A Critical Edition of
the Eighteenth Century Vocal Settings

Title page of the 1732 edition.

THE FABLES OF LA FONTAINE

A Critical Edition of the
Eighteenth-Century Vocal Settings

by

John Metz

JUILLIARD PERFORMANCE GUIDES No. 2

PENDRAGON PRESS   New York

The Juilliard Performance Guides

A Scholarly Series for the Practical Musician

Library of Congress Cataloging in Publication Data

Metz, John.
  The fables of La Fontaine.

  (Juilliard performance guides; no. 2)
  Originally presented as part of the author's thesis (D.M.A.-Juilliard School, 1980) under title: Fables from the Nouvelles poésies. Part one, Historical background and performance considerations.
  Bibliography: p.
  1. Fables sur de petits airs et des vaundevilles choises. 2. Songs, French–18th century–History and criticism. 3. Songs with continuo–18th century–History and criticism. 4. La Fontaine, Jean de, 1621–1695–Musical settings–History and criticism. I. Title. II. Series.
  ML2527.3.M47   1986   7843   83-8272
  ISBN 0-918728-26-6

Contents

Preface

"He is the toy of children, the mentor of youth, the friend of grown man."[1] With these words Charles Batteaux praised La Fontaine and his immortal *Fables* — those witty apologues which had entertained and enlightened the young and the old since they first appeared in 1680, and which are still read by school children in many lands.

In 1730, Paris received the first volume (Recueil) of the *Nouvelles Poésies Spirituelles et Morales sur les plus beaux Airs de la Musique Françoise et Italienne, avec une Basse continue,* a series of musical parodies that grew to eight volumes by 1737. At the end of the first six volumes of the *Nouvelles Poésies* there appeared a selection of the *Fables* of La Fontaine, set to vaudeville tunes and other simple airs. These *Fables* were apparently the most popular part of the *Nouvelles Poésies,* since they were issued separately in 1732 — before the final volumes of the *Nouvelles Poésies* even appeared. In the present study I have transcribed the music of the 1732 publication in order to make it more readable, and I have attempted to provide the information necessary for performance. Where not otherwise noted, the translations in this study are those of the author.

These delightful little songs have not been entirely passed over in the twentieth century, for Hugues Cuenod and Albert Fuller recorded seven of the *Fables* some years ago, for Cambridge Records.[2] Since that attractive recording was part of the inspiration for this edition, my thanks go to both artists, with special appreciation to Albert Fuller for the help he has given me over many years.

Others have assisted along the way. I am indebted to the Aston Magna Academies; Dr. Barry Brook; Dr. Susan Motherway, whose scholarship in French literature was always helpful; and to sopranos Daureen Podenski and Carol Wilson, who joined me in recent performances of the *Fables.*

1 Charles Batteaux, *Cours de belle-lettres* (1763) trans. and cited in Thomas Noel, *Theories of the Fable in the Eighteenth Century* (New York & London: Columbia University Press, 1975) 77.
2 "Songs from Shakespeare, Bach, and La Fontaine," perf. by Hughes Cuenod, tenor, and Albert Fuller, harpsichord (Cambridge Records CRS 1702).

PART ONE

Historical Background and Performance Considerations

I.

The Parody Principle —
Fables From The Nouvelles Poésies

In 1730 the publishing company of G. Desprez and J. Dessartz issued volume one (Premier Recueil) of the *Nouvelles Poésies Spirituelles et Morales sur les plus beaux Airs de la Musique Françoise et Italienne, avec une Basse continue.* This eight-volume set of solo songs was completed by 1737 by another publisher, Ph. N. Lottin and J. Butard, and reissued by the same company in 1752. The collection consisted of well-known French and Italian music, to which new words of a spiritual and moral quality had been added.[3] Although the present study centers on a separate publication of the *Fables* from the *Nouvelles Poésies*, I will first discuss the larger collection as a whole, in order to put the *Fables* into context.

The music of the *Nouvelles Poésies* — except for that of the *Fables* — is taken from works by some thirty composers, including Lully, Campra, Montéclair, Clérabault, Desmarets, Bacilly, and François Couperin. The melodies were taken from vocal and instrumental works, including cantatas, violin airs, musettes, and harpsichord and viol pieces. All of it is arranged for solo voice and continuo. Most of the airs appear to be for soprano or tenor voice; the remaining ones lie generally in the baritone range. There is no indication of who wrote the verses which were fitted to these airs. The "Avertissement" in the 1730 edition only tells us that, "Il suffit d'avertir que la Poésie est d'un grand Maître." As for the figured bass, the "Avis" states: "Les Basses ont été chiffrées avec grand soin par M. Clérambault [Louis-Nicolas Clérambault, 1676-1749], en faveur des Personnes qui accompagnent du Clavecin ou du Tuorbe." Each volume contains several written-out doubles "dans le goût de M. Lambert," on airs by Lully, Bacilly, Campra, and

---

[3] The practice of putting new words to older music was hardly new, the *contrafacta* of the thirteenth, and the *parody mass* of the sixteenth centuries are but two examples. The general term for such text-replacement is *parody*, a word which implies satire or caricature, though in the case of parodies with religious texts, this connotation is inappropriate.

others.[4] These provide us with complete examples of the practice of ornamenting the second and subsequent verses of French airs.

This collection was apparently written for all lovers of music, including children, for the same "Avertissement" indicates:

> We have added airs in which the words would not alarm Piety, and which have enough charm to be of equal interest to everyone. We hope thus to have rendered some service to young people who, with good reason, forbid all profane songs, but which good-naturedness sometimes obliges to sing at gatherings. The Fables which are at the end of the book may serve the same practice.[5]

In addition, the "Avis" mentions that the music is arranged with few page turns, "...which is no small matter for those who sing and play an instrument at the same time."

The volumes of the *Nouvelles Poésies* are divided into several sections, each one limited to a different religious topic. Volumes one through six include: *Louanges de Dieu, Misteres de Notres Seigneur, J.C., Vertus, Vices, Les IV Fins de l'Homme*, and *Fables*. As far as I can determine, volumes seven and eight were printed without *Fables*. RISM B II lists the volumes of the *Nouvelles Poésies* according to their original pagination, which numbered the *Fables* separately. (Vol. I: 72 –16p., Vol. II: 72 –16p., Vol. III: 44 –9p., Vol. IV: 44 –12p., Vol. VI: 44 –12p., Vol. VII: 56p., Vol. VIII: 56 p.)[6] Note that there is no entry of *Fables* in volumes VII and VIII. The separate 1732 edition of the *Fables* is also divided into volumes, and ends at volume six.

The title pages of the *Nouvelles Poésies* varied somewhat from volume to volume. The 1730 edition reads,"Nouvelles Poésies Spirituelles et Morales/sur/Les plus beaux Airs/de/la/Musique Françoise et Italienne/Avec une Basse continue." Although this volume does include the *Fables*, this fact is not mentioned on the main title page. The *Fables* have their own title page, which follows the first sections of the work. This additional title page reads, "Fables/sur/de Petits Airs/et/des Vaudevilles Choisis/avec/une Basse en Musette." By Vol. IV (1737) the two title pages were combined. Similarly, when the entire collection was reprinted in 1752, the title page read, "Nouvelles Poésies/Spirituelles et Morales/Sur/Les plus beaux Airs/de la/Musique Françoise et Italienne/Avec une Basse continue/On y joint/Des Fables Choisis/dans le Goût de M. De La Fontaine/Sur des Vaudevilles et petits airs/aisés à chanter, avec leur Basse &/une Basse en Musette."

The lengthy "Avertissement" published with *Nouvelles Poésies* was not reprinted in the separate edition of the *Fables*, but nevertheless it sheds some light on the editor's intentions:

---

[4] Presumably Michel Lambert (1610-1696).

[5] "On y a joint des airs, dont les paroles ne peuvent allarmer la Pieté, et qui ont assez d'agrement pour interesser indifferement tout le monde. On a cru par là rendu quelque service à de jeunes Persones qui s'interdisent avec raison toute chanson profane; mais que la complaissance oblige quelquefois de chanter en compagnie. Les fables qui sont à la fin de ce Livre peuvent servir au même usage."

[6] *Répertoire International des Sources Musicales,* pub. by the International Musicological Society and the International Association of Music Libraries (München-Duisburg: G. Henle, 1964) Vol. B II, 268.

One will find at the end of this work a collection of selected Fables on little airs and well-known vaudevilles, on the behalf of children. To make these more agreeable to them, a "Basse en Musette" has been added, which is very easy to play on the harpsichord, or any other instrument. We consider ourselves happy if in giving them an attraction for useful lessons which are suited to their age, we have given them an aversion to the profane songs which are often put into their mouths, and which only serve to corrupt their innocence.[7]

The *Nouvelles Poésies* was reviewed in a six-page article in the January 1730 edition of the *Mercure de France*. (The complete text of this important review may be found in Appendix B.) There was lavish praise for the poetry and the suitability of each air to its text. The reviewer expressed his hope that the collection as a whole would encourage people to make use of their voices, and not refuse when others ask them to sing. Special mention went to the *Fables*, "qui sont destinées principalement â fournir aux Enfans un amusement utile & convenable à leur âge." The final paragraph merits translation here.

> Without wanting to prejudice the judgement of the public, this collection seems to us to be an excellent mixture of the useful and the agreeable. A tender and solid piety, the noble thoughts, the unaffected (le naïf) quality of the Fables, and the choice and variety of the Airs — perfectly matched to the words: all equally invite those who shun vain amusements or dangerous pleasures in music. One could scarcely please them better: the beauty of the printing and the paper, and the moderate price are enough proof that those who undertook this collection only had the best interests of the public in mind.[8]

As I have said above, the music of the *Nouvelles Poésies* (excluding the *Fables*) all came from works by well-known and identifiable composers. An index was provided with each volume so that one could find out, for example, that "Bergers, reprenez vos musettes" (Vol. I, p. 34) is set to music by Clérambault. However, the music of the *Fables* is not indexed by composer. Each of the first two volumes concludes with a table, which indentifies each air by a short line of text — which appears to come from the vaudeville repertoire. Volumes three through six omit the table; instead the inscriptions appear just above each air, e.g. "Sur l'Air, Quelque vent qui gronde." (See plate 3, Appendix A.) There are four exceptions in which the tune is identified otherwise: Vol. I, Air III, "L'etoit un petit l'Anche (Noel Suisse)"; Vol. III, Air I, "Branle de Metz"; Vol. III, Air IV, "La Pastorelle de Monsieur Couperin"; Vol. III, Air VIII, "Noel de M Pélégrin." With these four exceptions, the lines of text appear appear to be *timbres* from the vaudeville.

According to Anthony:

---

[7] "On trouvera à la suite de cet Ouvrage un recueil de fables choisis sur les petits airs et vaudevilles les plus connus, en faveur des Enfans: et pour les leur rendre plus agréables on y a joint une Basse en Musette, qu'il leur sera tres facile de jouer sur le Clavecin, ou tant autre instrument. On s'estimeroit heureux si en leur donnant au l'attrait pour des leçons utiles et qui conviennent a leur age, on pouvait les dégouter de tant de chansons profanes qu'on leur met souvent dans la bouche, et qui ne servent qu'a corrompre leur innocence."

[8] *Mercure de France* (Jan 1730) 118–19. Original appears in Appendix B.

A *vaudeville* was any song whose melody had long since passed into public domain. It was indentified textually by a *timbre* which was a title usually based on the first line of the refrain by which the original tune was generally known. The entire melody of the song, tagged by this *timbre*, was known as a *fredon*. The tunes were folk-like with repeated, simple rhythmic patterns and a narrow melodic range; they were popularly called 'Pont Neuf tunes' after the famous bridge over the Seine which, because of its great width, was a favourite meeting-place for local minstrels. Any tune that caught the public's fancy was a likely candidate for the growing stockpile of *fredons*. Many of the simpler tunes from Lully's operas, such as 'Dans ces lieux tout rit sans cesse' from Phaëton, lived far into the eighteenth century as *fredons*.[9]

Much of the music used in the Comédie Italienne in France was made up of such vaudeville tunes, and the early Opéra Comique (1715–c. 1737) employed the same traditional melodies. At the foundation of this vaudeville system was a great national treasury of popular tunes, which were generally not identified by composer, and which could be used over and over again to convey a wide range of stories and emotions.

As Anthony has pointed out, it required talent to make a good match between text and tune.

> Le Sage and above all Favert (playwrights for the Théâtre de la Foire and the Opéra Comique, respectively) were very skillful in choosing among the vast stockpile of *vaudeville* tunes. A specific *fredon* was often employed in the same situation from one play to the next and functioned somewhat as a primitive leitmotif technique. Speaking of Favert's gift for *fredon* selection, Parfaict noted: 'These vaudevilles translate with minute exact successive degrees of the same sentiment and the most rapid, minute shifts within one action. Thus, the sleep of a shepherdess and the pursual of a kiss could scarcely be rendered with such delicate truth by newly composed music.[10]

It is not the purpose of this study to identify all the airs in all of the *Fables*, or even to determine how many of these melodies come from the vaudeville. However, the following illustration compares two of the airs from the *Fables* with their vaudeville counterparts, as indexed in *La Clé du Caveau*.[11]

---

[9] James R. Anthony, *French Baroque Music*, revised edition (New York: Norton, 1978) 153. The etymology of *vaudeville* is not clear. "There is no compelling documentation for the statement found in many eighteenth century sources that a certain Olivier Basselin, a fuller from Normandy, invented the *vaudeville*." Anthony, *loc. cit.* Other sources derive the word from *vaux de ville* (voices of the town) or *à vau de ville* (all about the town).

[10] *Ibid.*, 156-57. The quote is from Claude and François Parfaict, *Dictionnaire des théâtres de Paris*, 7 vols, (Paris 1756, reprint of 1767–70 ed., Geneva 1971) VI, 69.

[11] Pierre Adolphe Capelle, *La Clé du Caveau* (Paris: d'Abel Lanoi, 1816). This book indexes 1500 tunes by timbre. There were other such indexes e.g. *Le Théatre de la faire* (Paris, 1734–37).

(A) "Adieu paniers, vendanges sont faites," also known as, "Profitez bien, jeunes fillettes," as it appears in *La Clé du Caveau* (transposed from G Major).

(B) "Adieu paniers...." as used for "Le Mulet entêté de sa Noblesse" Vol. IV, Fable XIII, Air VIII.

(A) "Un sot qui veut l'habile," as it appears in *La Clé du Caveau* (transposed from G Minor).

(B) "Un sot qui...." as used for "La Cour de Lion" Vol. IV, Fable X, Air VI.

The melodies appear in slightly different versions in the two publications. "Adieu paniers..." varies only in touches of ornamentation. "Un sot..." has more dotted notes in the 1816 version, something which might indicate that it was usually sung dotted, and that the notation only became explicit after the heyday of the vaudeville. The second phrase of "Un sot.." differs in both pitch and rhythm. Perhaps the arranger of the *Fables* consciously changed the original tune in order to suit the words of "La Cour du Lion." On the other hand, these melodies were traditional, and changes could have easily occurred in time.

The following is "La Pastorelle" by François Couperin, compared with its version of the *Fables*. Notice that the arranger of the *Fables* eliminated the idiomatic harpsichord passage-work, and made the melody more folk-like.[12]

[12] François Couperin, "La Pastorelle," *Premier Ordre* in *Pièces de Clavecin, Premier Livre,* ed. Kenneth Gilbert (Paris: Heugel & Co., 1972) 23.

L'ASTROLOGUE, OUI SE LAISSE TOMBER DANS UN PUITS (Vol. III, Fable IV)

II.

The Fables of La Fontaine

Jean de La Fontaine was born at Château-Thierry on July 8, 1621. By the time his first set of *Fables* was published he had already established his reputation with several poems (the best-known being *Elégie aux nymphes de Vaux*), and with three collections of licentious tales (*Nouvelles en vers*, 1665; *Contes et nouvelles*, 1664–1671; and *Psyché*, 1669.) The first volume of the *Fables* was divided into six books, and was dedicated to the seven-year-old Dauphin in 1668. Encouraged by the success of this volume, La Fontaine published an additional book of *Fables* in 1671, two more in 1678, and three in 1679. In 1683 he was elected to the French Academy. He died on April 14, 1695.

In our time we do not seem to recognize the literary merits of La Fontaine's *Fables*. The ones we read in our youth are often forgotten before we are old enough to learn much from them. Yet this genre, rooted in classical Greece and Rome, has been honored by literary men for thousands of years. "Plato regarded poetry as detrimental to the public good and would have banned all forms from his republic except the fable, which he considered morally beneficial."[13] The first fabulist we know of was Aesop (sixth century B.C.E.), a Greek slave whose practical wisdom was transmitted orally for several hundreds of years until it was written down by various poets, including Phaedrus (30 B.C.E. to 44 C.E.), who translated Aesop into Latin iambic verse. As for La Fontaine, in the early eighteenth century, "...many respected critics even asserted that La Fontaine combined the sublimest quality of both Aesop and Phaedrus, the most eminent fabulists that the Greeks and Romans had to offer."[14]

Fables have had a long history in the education of youth. In the Renaissance those of Phaedrus were memorized by school children in the course of their instruction in Latin. In the eighteenth century, fables were an important element in moral instruction as well. "Common opinion considered moral instruction the paramount

---

[13] Thomas Noel, *Theories of the Fable in the Eighteenth Century* (New York & London: Columbia University Press, 1975) 4.

[14] *Ibid.*, 3.

pedagogical obligation and expected literature to assist in discharging it. A firm underlying moral, therefore, was required of all literature."[15] Thus the didactic quality of the fable was ideally suited to the educational philosophy of the day. La Fontaine, in his publication of 1669,

> ...maintains that the purpose is to assist in the formation of judgement and morals, especially in children, as well as to impart knowledge, specifically of the characters and properties of animals. Understanding of animals, he points out, advances understanding of oneself, since man 'summarizes all the good and bad in brute creatures.'[16]

La Fontaine drew on many sources. The majority of his *Fables* came from Aesop, whose works he knew through the translations of Phaedrus; others came from Babruis (Greek poet of the third century), the humanist Abstemius (Italian fabulist of the sixteenth century), and several other writers. La Fontaine did more than just translate the Aesop or Phaedrus fables; he transformed them. What had been dry and didactic became descriptive and imaginative. He infused them with a singular charm which he called "gaîté."

> Each fable seems a little self-contained world, where, beneath the apparent naiveté of talking animals, philosophizing oak trees, long-suffering woodcutters and millers, and the like, the voice of classical French clarity and good sense speaks in unmistakable accents.[17]

But the readership of fables was not limited to children. Various fables appeared in the *Mercure de France*, and "In France and Germany the fable invariably received detailed treatment in works on theory or principles of literature, treatises on *belles-lettres*, and encylopedias of the arts."[18]

In fact, Jean-Jacques Rousseau felt that La Fontaine's *Fables* were not at all suited to young children. In his play *Émile*, this writer-philosopher presented his belief that there was a complexity and immorality within the *Fables*, one which he felt would only bewilder youngsters. Rousseau recognized that the *Fables* had some pedagogical value, but he felt that children under fifteen were too young to understand these sophisticated abstractions, and would be confused by stories of talking dogs and conniving ducks. He sensed that "The morality in La Fontaine . . . consorts with such an admixture of immorality that it would be just as likely to inspire them to vice as to virtue."[19] Rousseau illustrated his point with *Le Corbeau et le Renard* (Vol. I, Fable II in the *Fables* of the *Nouvelles Poésies*). This is the story of the Crow who is perched on a tree with some cheese in his beak. The Fox comes along and so flatters the bird that he crows out in delight, and drops the cheese. The intended moral seems to be that one should be aware of false flatterers. But Rousseau was afraid that young children would mistake the point and side with the cun-

[15] *Ibid.*, 5.

[16] *Ibid.*, 11. Thomas Noel's translation.

[17] Bruce A. Morrissette, "La Fontaine," *Collier's Encyclopedia*, 24 vols. (U.S.: Crowell-Collier Educational Corporation, 1969) XIV, 253.

[18] Noel, 11.

[19] *Ibid.*, 4.

ning Fox. As Thomas Noel put it, "Should a six-year-old child be introduced to people who flatter and lie for the sake of gain?"[20] Yet Rousseau deemed the *Fables* valuable for older children, for "Now he (the older child) can understand the fox's cunning flattery of the crow because he has been a victim of flattery himself."[21] Whether or not we agree with Rousseau's educational philosophy, we can admire his insight into the *Fables*. He recognized that La Fontaine's morality was a complex one—one which reflected the sophistication of French intellect.

In many cases La Fontaine is really only a fanciful re-telling of Aesop or Phaedrus. The usual difference is that where Aesop just relates the story in a matter-of-fact way, La Fontaine dresses his tale with descriptive narrative. Another contribution was that La Fontaine used free verse in his *Fables* so that the shape of the meter would contribute to the feeling of the story.

In some cases he truly transformed Aesop's fable, giving it a less orthodox moral. The following example presents three versions of the story of the Grasshopper and the Ant, (1) as it appears in Aesop, (2) in La Fontaine, and (3) in the musical *Fables* of 1732. It is obvious that the arranger of the *Fables* rewrote La Fontaine's version to fit the metrical structure of the vaudeville.

The Ant and the Grasshopper

In a field one summer's day a Grasshopper was hopping about, chirping and singing to its heart's content. An Ant passed by, bearing along with great toil an ear of corn he was taking to the nest.

"Why not come and chat with me," said the Grasshopper, "instead of toiling and moiling in that way?"

"I am helping to lay up food for the winter," said the Ant, "and recommend you to do the same."

"Why bother about winter?" said the Grasshopper; "we have got plenty of food at present." But the Ant went on its way and continued its toil. When the winter came the Grasshopper had no food, and found itself dying of hunger, while it saw the ants distributing every day corn and grain from the stores they had collected in the summer. Then the Grasshopper knew:

"IT IS BEST TO PREPARE FOR THE DAYS OF NECESSITY"[22]

La Cigale et la Fourmi	*The Cicada and the Ant**
La Cigale, ayant chanté	The Cicada, having sung
Tout l'Été,	all summer long,
Se trouva fort dépourvue	Found herself destitute
Quand la bise fut venue.	When the north wind came.
Pas un seul petit morceau	Not a single bit
De mouche ou de vermisseau.	Of a fly or a maggot.

---

[20] *Ibid.,* 107.

[21] *Ibid.,* 108.

[22] *Folk-Lore and Fable—Aesop, Grimm, Andersen,* from the *Harvard Classics,* edited by Charles W. Eliot (New York: P.F. Collier & Son, 1937) 25–26.

* Author's translation.

Elle alla crier famine
Chez la Fourmi sa voisine,
La priant de lui preter
Quelque grain pour subsister
Jusqu'à la saison nouvelle.
Je vous paierai, lui dit-elle,
Avant l'Oût, foi d'animal,
Interet et principal.
La Fourmi n'est pas prêteuse;
C'est là son moindre défaut.
"Que faisiez-vous au temps chaud?
Dit-elle à cette emprunteuse.
—Nuit et jour à tout venant
Je chantais, ne vous déplaise.
— Vous chantiez?
    j'en suis fort aise.
Eh bien! dansez maintenant."[23]

She went crying "Famine"
To the Ant's place — her cousin,
Entreating her to loan her
Some grain for subsistance
Until the new season.
"I will pay you,"she told her,
"Before August, Animal's Honor,
Interest and principal."
The Ant was no lender:
That was the least of her shortcomings.
"What did you do when it was warm?"
She said to the borrower.
"—Night and day, I sang
For all who came, don't be displeased."
"—You sang?
    I'm *so* pleased.
Ah well! Now dance."

    La Fourmi, et la Sauterelle — "L'Oisiveté"
Pendant l'été. Chante et bondit la Sauterelle:
    Pendant l'été.
On la voit dans l'oisiveté:
Mais au Travail prompte et fidelle,
La fourmi ne fait pas comme elle,
    Pendant l'été.
Pendant l'hiver. La Sauterelle est sans pitance:
    Pendant l'hiver.
Elle est réduite a vivre d'air:
Et la Fourmi dans l'abondance,
Lui dit: belle chanteuse danse,
    Pendant l'hiver.

    The Ant and the Grasshopper — "Laziness"
During the summer. The Grasshopper sang and bounded
    During the summer.
One saw her being lazy.
But prompt and faithful to her work,
The Ant didn't do as *she* did,
    During the summer.
During the winter. The Grasshopper was poor
    During the winter.
She was reduced to living on air.
So the Ant in her abundance told her:
Lovely singer, now dance,
    During the winter.

[23] Jean de La Fontaine, *Fables* (Paris: Garnier-Flammarion, 1966) 51.

III.

Performance Considerations

FOR THE SINGER

It is outside the scope of this paper to treat in depth every aspect of French Baroque vocal performance, as there are many extensive studies which examine each specific concern in detail (notes inegales, pronunciation, etc.). However, it seems in order to make a few general comments on style, and to offer a series of guidelines concerning performance of the *Fables*, based on contemporary sources, and my own experience in attempting to recreate these works.

One might argue that some of the refinements suggested in this chapter would be beyond the training and ability of a typical eighteenth-century amateur. However, good performers have always been well versed in the style of their own era, and in the eighteenth century at least, there was a discriminating public which had a fairly high standard of musicianship.

In addition, the following discussion may seem overly slanted towards an elegance of performance inappropriate to vaudevilles. For example, one might quote Jean-Jacques Rousseau in arguing for a more folk-like rendering of the *Fables*.

> The tune of the *vaudevilles* is usually not very musical. As one only pays attention to the words, the tune only serves to make the recitation more stressed; moreover one usually feels neither taste, nor tune, nor meter. The *vaudeville* belongs exclusively to the French, and they are in that very lively and very pleasant.[24]

I would point out, however, that La Fontaine's works reflect his association with

---

[24] Jean-Jacques Rousseau, "Vaudeville," *Dictionnaire de Musique* (Paris: 1768) 531–32. "L'Air des *vaudevilles* est communément peu musical, Comme on n'y fait attention qu'aux paroles. L'Air ne sert qu'à rendre la récitation un peu plus appuyée; du reste on n'y sent pour l'ordinaire ni goût, ni Chant, ni Mesure. Le *vaudeville* appartient exclusivement aux François, & ils en ont de très-piquans & de très-plaisants."

persons of very high rank, including the minister Fouquet, the Duchesse de Bouillon, and the Marquise de la Sablière. His *Fables* are far superior to the verses commonly found in the vaudeville; many of them are certainly more than merely "de très-piquans & de très-plaisants."

Thus the parodies found in the musical *Fables* of 1732 lie somewhere between folk art and cultivated music. A convincing performance, then as well as today, would probably be a mixture of sophisticated performance standards as well as the more bawdy atmosphere of the Théâtre de la foire. Such a performance must be thoroughly French, and should suggest the atmosphere of a Parisian salon.

First of all, any singer who is not experienced in eighteenth-century French music should keep in mind the basic differences between the French and Italian styles of the period. Anthony has compiled a list of adjectives which describe French and Italian music from a *French* point of view. His list, culled from French treatises of 1636 to 1746, includes under the description of French music: "beauté, calme, charme, délicate, douceur, élégant, grâce, intelligent, naturel, netteté, noble, régularité, (la belle) simplicité, tendresse, and touchant." The contrasting list (still culled from French texts) yields: "baroque, brilliant, bruit, chargé, colère, défigure, dépit, détourne, diversité, excès, extravagance, fureur, gaieté, licence, peu naturel, rage, recherché, savant, singulier, variété, vif, violence, vivacité."[25]

A major difference which this list does not point out is that the relationship between words and music in France was very different from that found in Italy. Under influence of the Comédie Française, French poetry had taken on the structure of classical metrical verse — a development far removed from any Italian practice, and one which had far-reaching effects on singing in France. This *vers-mesuré* was an adaption of the principles of ancient Greek prose. "French remained the only European language in which quantitative values (syllable length) played an important role in vocal declamation."[26] The recitation style of the Comédie Française was equidistant between speech and song, and was copied by French composers. Bénigne de Bacilly, in *Remarques curieuses sur l'art de bien chanter*, makes several comments about the relationship betweeen singing and poetic meter:

> ...in addition to the freedom which is permissible in Italian, as exemplified by the elisions of syllables, which can be used to shorten words whenever one wishes (which is never allowed in French), it is permissible to repeat Italian words at any length that happens to please the composer.[27]

The third part of Bacilly's book is entitled "The Application of vocal music to French words, with regard to their length." It draws attention to the importance of considering syllable length when reciting French poetry.

[25] James R. Anthony, *French Baroque Music*, revised edition (New York: Norton, 1978) 113.
[26] Vincent Duckles, review of *A Commentary upon The Art of Proper Singing* by Bénigne de Bacilly (Paris: 1668) translated and edited by Austin B. Caswell (New York: The Institute of Mediaeval Music Ltd., 1968) *M.L.S. Notes* XXIV/3 (March 1970) 527–28.
[27] Bénigne de Bacilly, *A Commentary upon The Art of Proper Singing* (Paris: 1668) translated and edited by Austin B. Caswell (New York: The Institute of Mediaeval Music Ltd., 1968) 42 [92]. Pagination in brackets is from original publication.

One must certainly agree....that French poetry takes no cognizance of the length of syllables *insofar as it is written* as long as some rhyme is maintained; but when it comes to the question of *reciting, singing, or declaiming* some verse in a proper fashion, it is obvious that differing syllable length must be observed not only in poetry but also in prose.

....Since vocal music is a kind of declamation, as I have mentioned before, there can be no doubt that one must have a great deal of concern for the length of syllables without which vocal music is drastically impaired.[28]

Bacilly's main thesis is that the singer should never transgress against natural syllable length. Ornaments can sometimes be used to add length to a long syllable, but should generally not be added to a short one, as that would distort the proper proportion within the poetic line. This distortion would not only bend the rules of good declamation, it would also make the text less clear to the listener. Yet composers sometimes overlooked the proper stress of syllables, and even when they were careful of it, the second (and subsequent) verses of a strophic air would require some adjustments (often done through added ornamentation) so that the syllables and text would not be distorted. Bacilly explains this further in a chapter which happens to be about monosyllables; the principle could definitely be applied to the *Fables*, and not only to monosyllables.

It is certainly true that the arrangement of long and short monosyllables in the first verse sets the rhythm patterns of the melody; and if it occurs that in the subsequent verse conflicting patterns arise which cannot be easily accommodated within the given melodic rhythms, it is up to the singer to remedy this conflict as best he can through his industry and training.[29]

In French Baroque music in general, and especially in the *Fables*, one must take care not to sing "too well." Italianate beauty of line is less important here than the singer's ability to convey the meaning of each word and every contrast implied in the text. Bacilly in fact prefers a *good* voice to a *pretty* one:

A single tone of a *pretty* voice is very pleasing to the ear because of its clearness and sweetness, and above all because of the nice vibrato which usually accompanies it. The good voice on the other hand, may not have all this sweetness and natural vibrato, but nevertheless is effective because of its vigor, strength, and its capacity to sing with expression, which is the soul of vocal art.[30]

Small voices, he says, "...have a great advantage over big ones, in that they have greater flexibility for the performance of vocal agréments, since the vocal chords are more delicate and therefore more suitable for slurring over certain tones which ought not be accented."[31]

---

[28] *Ibid.*, 175 [328].
[29] *Ibid.*, 185 [351].
[30] *Ibid.*, 20 [38].
[31] *Ibid.*, 22 [44].

Here again there is a similarity with the tradition of the Comédie Française, for this rhetorical style, truly French in spirit, can present changes of feeling and sensitivities which are as ephemeral as a gust of wind. As a person can shiver with fear, sigh with longing, smile with anticipation, so can French airs reflect a delicate kaleidoscope of emotions. Nowhere could these marked contrasts be more useful than in the various dialogues between the members of the animal kingdom in La Fontaine's *Fables*.

Recordings of the Comédie Française can be very helpful to the singer. Their recording of *Polyeucte*, for example, is a model of French declamation.[32]

PRONUNCIATION

In the refined atmosphere of mid-eighteenth-century French culture, no attribute was more important to singing than a careful and expressive pronunciation. Bénigne de Bacilly, in the seventeenth century, had devoted two-thirds of his book to pronunciation and to the differences between everyday speech and vocal performance.

> But since, at present, it seems that vocal music has reached the highest degree of perfection that it is possible to achieve, it is not enough merely to pronounce words clearly—it is also necessary to do so with the necessary force. Thus, it is incorrect to claim that a singer ought to sing his words just as he speaks them unless one also adds "in public" to the statement. The singer must avoid the type of pronunciation used in familiar speech as will be made quite apparent by what follows.[33]

Because classical French singers put so much emphasis on pronunciation, today's singers should be equally careful, even when doing such informal music as the *Fables*. They should be aware of the changes in pronunciation and spelling from eighteenth-century to current French. Now here a difficulty may arise, for if today one sings *i parl* for *il parl* (il parle), or *trubler* when today one would sing *truble* (troubler), someone in the audience is going to get upset.[34] But the fact remains that old French was pronounced differently, and that for a truly stylistic performance such differences must be taken into account. Perhaps some accommodations may be made for the modern audience, but those adjustments should be made only after the original pronunciation has been studied.

To the reader who wants to be well informed on the topic, I would recommend Jean-Baptiste Bérard's book, *L'Art du chant*; Bacilly's *Remarques curieuses sur*

---

[32] Corneille, excerpts from *Polyeucte — Tragedy in Five Acts*, performed by the Comédie Française (Period Records FRL 1507). Not all performances of the Comédie Francaise are equal to that on this recording. In the opinion of some critics, their performance of Molière's *Le Misanthrope* in New York (1979) was stylistically poor, as traditional performance values had been corrupted by attempts at modernization.

[33] *Ibid.*, 130 [250].

[34] The phonetic symbols used in this study are those of the International Phonetic Association.

l'art de bien chanter; or, for an excellent digestion of many treatises, Sally Sanford's paper, *A Guide to Singing the French Language According to the Principles in Seventeenth- and Eighteenth- Century Treatises.*[35] What follows here is largely extracted from her paper and from Bacilly, and represents what I feel are the major exceptions to modern pronunciation.

1) ã ɔ̃ ɛ̃

For the ã, which is pronounced like a nasalized open o (ɔ), Bacilly says:

It is advisable not to pronounce the *n* at the beginning, rather to save it until near the end of the note—especially when it is a long one. If the syllable occurs over a number of notes (as in *Ports de Voix, Diminutions,* and in *Tremblements*, which always contain more than a single note), the *n* should not be pronounced at all until the end of the final note has been reached, since the *n* cannot be sung in any way other than with a nasal tone.[36]

For the ɔ̃ he does not advise delaying the nasalization, but suggests instead, "...but in the *on* the singer must insert a subtle element of the *u.*"[37] Bérard and Raparlier, however, do recommend delaying the nasalization.

For the ɛ̃ Sanford recommends also delaying the nasalization, thus prolonging the open e (ɛ).

2) *l* in "il"

Bacilly tells us that the final l was often dropped in common speech, but that it should always be pronounced in singing, *except in chansonnettes and vaudevilles.*

In my opinion, the *l* must be pronounced solidly, even in the monosyllable (il), for the purpose of giving the piece of music more solidity and weight. Of course, there are exceptions to this approach, especially in circumstances where weight and solidity have no place such as *Chansonnettes, Vaudevilles*, and other such bagatelles which must be sung with as little intensity as possible.[38]

3) *r*

The *r* was normally trilled in singing of this period, as noted in Lecuyer and Bérard. In addition, Bacilly insists on retaining some of the *r* sound at the end of infinitives, so that the meaning is made clear.

I....hold that it is a great mistake to obliterate this final *r* completely. Not only does declamation become flat and feeble without it, but also its removal may cause confusion as to word-meanings. A good example is [Here he cites a setting of "c'est un bien de celer"] ...if the *r* were to be omitted from *celer*, the meaning would become confused since it would sound like 'un bien de cele' rather than 'un bien de celer.'[39]

[35] Sally Sanford, "A Guide to Singing the French Language According to the Principles in Seventeenth- and Eighteenth-Century Treatises" (a term project submitted to the department of music of Stanford University, (1979.)

[36] Bacilly, *op. cit.*, 135 [261].

[37] *Ibid.*, 143 [276].

[38] *Ibid.*, 155 [299].

[39] *Ibid.*, 153 [296].

But he continues,

> At the opposite extreme it is an equally serious mistake to pronounce a strong *r* on the infinitives of all verbs, especially when the song doesn't warrant that kind of emphasis as, for example, in *vaudevilles*. In such cases, the singer must use prudence and take a middle course between two extremes, so that his pronunciation is neither too coarse nor too insipid.[40]

And he recommends matching the final *r*'s in rhyming lines such as:

> 'O l'excuse légère, d'un esprit trop léger,
> Pardonne à ton Berger.'[41]

4) z

Here Sanford's concise summation of Bacilly on this important matter is worth quoting in extenso:

> Bacilly and Raparlier indicate that final s was pronounced more frequently than in modern French. Depending on the word and whether it is followed by a word beginning with a vowel, final s will have the sound of s or z.
>
> Bacilly gives several guidelines for sounding a final s, all of which have the aim of making the text better understood. Bacilly states that is obligatory to sound the final s:

> 1) to distinguish the plural from the singular;
> 2) to avoid "cacaphony";
> 3) to make the text clear when the meaning would be altered if the s were not sounded;
> 4) when the following word begins with a vowel.

As an example of the first case, Bacilly gives the lines

> a. Fleurs qui naissez sous les pas de Silvie
> b. Les Fleurs qui naissent dans la plaine.

While the plural is indicated in line b by the definite article, the *s* in Fleurs must be sounded in line a because it has no plural indicator. A "cacaphony" results if the *s* is omitted from the past definite of the verb croire, crus, and thus becomes confused with the past participle, *cru*, as in the lines

> je crus en vous quittant
> j'ay cru on vous quittant.

As an example of making the meaning of the text clear, Bacilly cites the need for pronouncing both the *r* and *s* in the word *pensers* so that it is not confused with the feminine *pensées*.[42]

---

[40] *Ibid.*, 153 [296].
[41] *Ibid.*, 154 [298].
[42] Sanford, *op. cit.*, 46, 47.

5) oi, oy

This is the most vexing aspect of early French pronunciation, as the imperfect and conditional verb endings *oit* underwent a gradual spelling change in the early eighteenth century, before establishing the modern spelling *ait*. In the *Fables* one sees: "Dame Lion *avoit* un fils." The *avoit* should be pronounced more like our *avait*, that is **avɛ**, but perhaps a bit broader. There is some suspicion that the aristocracy said **avwɛ,** so the singer might imitate that pronunciation in any section of a fable which is a quote from someone of royalty (perhaps when the king of beasts speaks.)

Nouns such as loi, roi, etc. were once pronounced **lwɛ**, **rwɛ**, etc., especially at court.

Although the aristocracy centered around the court in the later seventeenth and early eighteenth centuries cultivated the **wɛ** sound, the general populace of Paris tended toward **wa**. By the time of Bérard's *L'Art du chant*, the latter pronunciation had come to be accepted for singing; only a few conservative aristocrats at court and members of the older generation still kept the **wɛ** pronunciation. While the Revolution brought about the final demise of most aristocratic pronunciation, Lafayette is said to have pronounced *le roi* as **lə rwɛ** on his visit to the United States as late as 1824.[43]

Thus again in singing the *Fables* one might reflect the status of the character in the choice of **wa** or **wɛ**. Vol. II, Fable V, verse III might be a good example. Here a presumptuous lawyer proclaims:

Voyons, puisque c'est à moi
De juger selon la loi

Perhaps an overstuffed comic effect would be obtained with **muwɛ** and **luwɛ**.

6) Consonants in general

The strength and length of consonants was often altered in order to underline the meaning of certain words and affects.

The laws which govern singers in this regard vary infinitely on account of the modifications to which they are susceptible. It is necessary to pay attention to all the degrees and all the nuances of the emotions. It is the function of sentiment to grasp them; it is for taste and art to render them. This latter renders pronunciation capable of imitating nature.[44]

To summarize this important aspect of pronunciation:

(A) For violent passions, vehement emotions—use a hard, dark—pronunciation, and strong stress or "doubling" of consonants.[45]

[43] Sanford, *op. cit.*, 35.
[44] Jean-Baptiste Bérard, *L'Art du chant*, (Paris: 1755) translated in new edition by Sidney Murray (Milwaukee: Pro Musica Press, 1969) 49-50. Quoted by Sanford on p. 11.
[45] *Ibid.*, 16.

Examples:

> *Les Membres et l'Estomac*, Vol. I, Fable XXVI
> "Qu'ils étoient *l*as de *t*ant *v*eiller,
> De *t*ant *t*ravailler"
> *Le Meunier, son Fils, et l'Ane*, Vol. II, Fable VIII
> "*La Bete est t*rop peu *f*orte pour deux."
> *La Vieille, et les deux Servantes*, Vol. III, Fable VII
> "Ah! *m*audit *C*oq, se dirent-elles, Tu *p*eriras":

(B) In sad, tearful passions Bérard suggests an "extremely dark" or almost "choked" pronunciation.[46]
Examples:

> *La Fourmi, et la Sauterelle*, Vol. I, Fable I
> "Elle est réduite à vivre d'air"
> *La Lice et sa Compagne*, Vol. I, Fable IX
> "Que mes foibles enfans
> Encore à la mamelle."

If these examples seem to be exaggerations of "sad and tearful passions," all the better, for the *Fables* thrive on overstatement.

In summary, it is clear that the singer must not only pronounce the language clearly and correctly, but that an element of artistic creativity and taste must be present in order to make the best effect.

ORNAMENTATION

Composers in this period were rarely explicit in their notation of ornaments. Most composers marked all their trills with a + , even though there were many different types of trill, each appropriate for a certain musical element. The performer must still use his taste and judgment, even when the composer has used one of the more specific trill signs ($\widehat{t}$, $\textit{w}$, t .) When the singer knows which notes are to make up the ornament, he must yet examine the *manner* of singing the notes—especially the dynamic inflections—which are particular to French ornamentation.

The following survey is intended as a demonstration of a palette of devices, a vocabulary of rhetorical ornaments which the singer will have to adapt to the *Fables*, and which he will need to apply in diverse ways when suitable.

PORTS DE VOIX (The Appoggiatura from Below)

The port de voix is usually shown by a small note (A), but sometimes by ⌄ (B). There were many types of ports de voix: port de voix entier, coulé, feint or double,

---

[46] *Ibid.*, 16.

fini, battu, and simple. Montéclair's treatise names only the port de voix, and notes that "The port de voix is not always marked in the places where it ought to be used; taste and experience give this knowledge."[47]

In general, "The port de voix...rises in a manner caressing or plaintive."[48] This seems to explain Bacilly's text, where he calls for a repetition of the upper note, which actually appears to be just a gentle accent (caress) which is felt after that note is first heard (C). I have not found that particular interpretation in treatises as late as the *Nouvelles Poésies*, but David, in 1737, tells us:

> The port de voix is one of the most essential matters in the neatness (propreté) of singing; it decorates in a manner so gracious that it can express all that the soul would feel...and few singers have tried to render it as touching and sensitive as it must be done; and it is only with the sentiments of a moved soul that one can be said to have attained perfection in this ornament.[49]

The port de voix feint merely refers to dwelling on the small note longer than in the ordinary port de voix. One often executes a mordant (D). The port de voix double fills in an ascending third (E). Of the port de voix in general, Jane Arger suggests:

> In tender or gracious airs, it would seem better to combine it with a vibrato (flatte) or a mordant (martellement) very legato and gently. In quick airs one rarely uses this ornament. In dramatic airs it would be better to use the port de voix feint.[50]

[47] Michel Pignolet de Montéclair, *Principes de musique, Divisez en quatre partis* (Paris, 1736). Translation of pp. 77–90 appears in Montéclair, *Cantatas for One and Two Voices*, edited by James R. Anthony and Diran Akmajian, from *Recent Researches in the Music of the Baroque Era* (Madison, Wis.: A-R Editions, Inc. 1978) xix.

[48] l'abbé Demotz de la Salle, quoted in Jane Arger, *Les Agréments et le rythme* (Paris: Rouart, Lerolle, et Cie., 1921) 30.

[49] François David, quoted in Arger, *op. cit.*, 31.

[50] Arger, *op. cit.*, 34.

COULÉ (passing note)

The coulé is generally a note which fills in the interval of a descending third. It is not always marked, but when it is, one finds a small note or several other markings (A). "When the words express anger, or when the song is in a precipitous movement, one does not use the coulé in descending thirds."[51] Its use in tender or langourous airs is suggested by Blanchet. "It expresses certain gracious or sad movements, and passions which are serious or loving."[52] There is some confusion about the placement of the small note, whether it should take time from the upper or lower note of the third (B) or (C). Here Kenneth Gilbert gives us some insight which relates to the importance of stressed and non-stressed syllables: The final mute 'e' which occurs on the weak endings of so many French words must never be accented. When a feminine word of this type ends a phrase, one often finds the formula of a descending third. Here one must put the coulé before the lower note, slurring to it. This removes the accent from the last note of the phrase, as in (C).[53]

ACCENT OR PLAINTE (the lift)

In contrast with the above ornaments, this one has neither rhythmic nor definite melodic value. It is a brief raising of pitch just before dropping to a lower note. It can be marked by a small note or by a ' . It seems that the accent need not be a complete half-step or full-step higher than the written note. As Loulié wrote in 1698, "The enharmonic system comprises natural and altered sounds, and also other sounds which musicians call 'plaintes,' in which 'plaintes' the semi-tones are divided into yet smaller intervals."[54] According to Montéclair:

> The accent is a mournful exhalation or elevation of the voice practiced more often in plaintive than in tender airs. It is never used in gay airs or in those which express anger.
> The sound is produced in the chest by a type of sob occurring at the end of a note of long duration or of a main note; this permits the scale step immediately above the accented note to be heard for an instant.[55]

TREMBLEMENT (the trill)

All singers have some ability to trill, but unfortunately many are content with only one trill, which they turn on and off as if it were a doorbuzzer. Instead, one needs a

[51] Montéclair, in Arger, *op. cit.*, 35.
[52] Blanchet, in Arger, *op. cit.*, 37.
[53] Kenneth Gilbert, "Introduction" of his edition of *Pièces de Clavecin* by François Couperin (Paris: Heugel, 1972) XVIII–XIX.
[54] Arger, *op. cit.*, 38.
[55] Montéclair, *op. cit.*, xix.

palette which includes slow and fast trills, accelerating trills, and trills with various terminations. This palette can be enhanced by varying degrees of distinctness in the two notes of the trill. Sometimes one should slur the notes in such a legato fashion that the trill becomes a gentle waver; other times it should be very precise in its pitches. Bacilly says, "Concerning a cadence [trill] which is too slow, it might be said that this deficiency is like the 'the bride being too beautiful,' since slowness in a cadence is an advantage provided that it gets a bit faster at the end than it was at the beginning."[56] He then notes that this slower trill is more appropriate at cadences, and that a faster trill is best for brightening notes within a phrase.

Montéclair gives four kinds of trill:[57]

t 1) The tremblement appuyé (prepared trill)

The first note of this trill (the appoggiatura) is long or short depending on context, but it is heard. "To perform a *tremblement* perfectly, one must prepare it well, and end it well. A *tremblement* is called 'pearly' when its beats are equal and make an agreeable effect in the throat."

+ 2) The tremblement subit (short trill)

This trill has no preparation (appoggiatura), and is more suited to recitatives than to airs.

⁀⁎ 3) The tremblement feint (incomplete)

This is generally prepared, but the trill itself has a very short duration. "The *tremblement feint* is employed when the sense of the words is incomplete or when the melody has not yet reached its conclusion."

⁀t 4) The tremblement doublé (trill with prefix.) (See example below.) "The *tremblement doublé* is often found in tender airs, where there are many passages marked by small notes, as one may see in the *doubles* of Lambert, Dambruis, and other earlier composers."

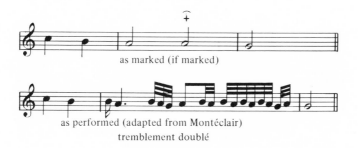

as marked (if marked)

as performed (adapted from Montéclair)
tremblement doublé

In spite of Montéclair's many different signs, the t is generally found for all trills, *especially in printed scores.* The singer must decide which trill is appropriate, and frequently has to add trills which are not marked in the music — principally at cadences, where their presence is assumed. Bacilly's advice is especially important: *Don't trill on short syllables.*

---

[56] Bacilly, *op. cit.*, 83 [166].
[57] Montéclair, *op. cit.*, xiv-xv.

CHÛTE (the descending anticipation)

The chûte is not mentioned by all authors, but Loulié gives us several examples (see below). Montéclair writes:

> The chûte is an inflection of the voice which after having sustained a note for some time, falls gently while permitting the sound to die away to a lower note without pausing there.
> The chûte is an important embellishment used in melodies of pathos.[58]

Jane Arger notes that the chûte is like our modern portamento, except that while for us it is equally expressive of sadness or gaiety, in the Baroque it seemed more limited to pathos.[59]

Chûte, Loulié from Arger p 42

MARTELLEMENT or *PINCÉ* (the mordant)

Singers in the eighteenth century generally used the word *martellement* for the same ornament that clavecinists called the *pincé* or *mordant*. It is the alternation of a main note with the note below, starting and ending on the main note. Some of the signs are shown below. Though there were varying interpretations, Jane Arger suggests that it be executed more or less rapidly, and that the grave character of an air can be brought out by a *port de voix* slurred up to a mordant. The mordant by itself is good for animating words, or for making them more gracious or lively.[60] Montéclair says it has no sign in vocal music.

Martellement, Loulié from Arger p 46

---

[58] Montéclair, *op. cit.*, xv.
[59] Arger, *op. cit.*, 43.
[60] Arger, *op. cit.*, 47.

FLATÉ, FLATTÉ, or *FLATEMENT* (the vibrato)

This is an ornament about which the authors are very unclear. "It is confused with the *port de voix*, combined with the *pincé*, or with the *pincé simple* or the *martellement* or the *balancement*...."[61] Montéclair describes it as a "type of vibrato which the voice makes by means of several small, gentle exhalations without raising or lowering the pitch."[62] On the other hand, Bérand writes:

> The flatté or the balancé requires a nearly imperceptible inflection of the voice; it requires furthermore that one rapidly join two notes higher and lower while governing the sound. One may regard this ornament as a quarter of a port de voix. After having given the principal note, take care to make the larynx raise a quarter of a degree and exhale softly in the interval of these two notes.[63]

The confusion of signs used to mark the flatté is so great that it seems best to simply realize that there are intermediate steps between two extremes: 1) a mordant which is clearly articulated with exact pitches, and 2) a less distinct ornament which approaches the vibrato. Dellain seems to have summed it up in 1781: "The flattés serve the tender expression...they are made by gliding together two or more notes, blending them like a little pincé or trembling."[64]

BALANCEMENT (the tremulo)

This is sometimes compared with the tremulo on the organ. "To execute it well, the voice must perform several small exhalations more marked and slower than those of the *flaté*."[65] It too is confused with the martellement and the flatté, but generally speaking it seems to be the least marked, the most delicate of the three. Lacassagne says, "There are also the martellements so insensible that one may only regard them as simple vibrations or shivers on a note; and thus one may mark them ~~~~ ."[66]

Do the flatté and the balancement involve pitch or volume fluctuation, or both? I do not think there is an answer here. Each singer must develop as wide and subtle a vocabulary as his voice will allow, and should reserve different amounts and intensities of vibrato for different expressive needs.

TOUR DE GOSIER (the turn)

The turn, indicated by the sign ∾, was not greatly different then from what it is today, though it was executed with more varied rhythmic and dynamic expression. Singers, especially, were more free in many ornaments than were instrumentalists. Montéclair gives the only exception to our customary interpretation of the turn,

---

[61] *Ibid.*, 48.
[62] Montéclair, *op. cit.*, xvi.
[63] Arger, *op. cit.*, 49.
[64] *Ibid.*, 49.
[65] Montéclair, *op. cit.*, xvi.
[66] Arger, *op. cit.*, 52.

when he prescribes a sudden tremblement on the second note of the turn (see below). "This ornament forms a warbling in the throat which is difficult to execute and still more difficult to explain."[67]

the Turn (after Montéclair)

HÉLAN or SANGLOT (the gasp or sob)

Montéclair gives the best description of the *sanglot*, which he says can be used to express many different passions. It originates in the chest with a violent release of the breath which makes a muffled sound before the actual note begins. The written note is then usually followed by an *accent* or a *chûte*.

> The sanglot is employed for the most acute suffering, for the greatest sadness, for laments, for tender melodies, for anger, for contentment, and even for joy.
> It is almost always used on the first syllable of the word "hélas!" and on the exclamations "ah!" "eh!"[68]

It seems to be a gutteral sound, and probably involves a glottal stop in its formation. There are no markings for it.

SON FILÉ, SON ENFLÉ ET DIMINUÉ, TRAIT, COULADE, SON GLISSÉ
(straight tones, crescendo and diminuendo, articulated and slurred runs, and the slide)

These are musical devices which we think of as general elements of expression, but which the eighteenth-century treatises categorized as specific vocal ornaments. Since these all pertain to *how* one uses the voice, they have been grouped together here.

Son enflé means a crescendo and decrescendo on a single note. Montéclair claims to have invented the markings ◀▶, though these were known before his time. The best approach today is for the singer to be aware that the crescendo-decrescendo is an ornament, and that it should be saved for special moments. Again, as with the tremulo and vibrato, one should first have an unadorned sound to which color can be added when needed. The unadorned, straight sound was called *son filé*. Of this Montéclair says, "The *son filé* is executed on

---

[67] Montéclair, *op. cit.*, xvi.
[68] Montéclair, *op. cit.*, xvii.

a note of long duration by sustaining the voice without the slightest bit of fluctuation. The voice must be, so to speak, as smooth as ice during the entire
duration of the note."[69]

Similarly, the difference between *trait* (articulated runs) and *coulade* (slurred runs) should be considered as an important source of expressive variety.
The *son glissé* is a slow, gradual change in pitch from one note to its neighbor.
Montéclair compares it to gliding one's foot along the floor, instead of picking
it up.[70]

PASSAGES OR DIMINUTIONS

Passages or diminutions are groups of quick notes, more or less arbitrarily
chosen, which embellish simpler melodic lines. Today they are commonly employed in the return of the 'A' section of Italian-style da capo arias, where
their main function is to heighten the intensity of the repeat. But free embellishment is also an essential element in French airs.

Loulié uses the word *passages* to refer to notes "which are intermingled
with simple ornaments," and he gives the following examples:[71]

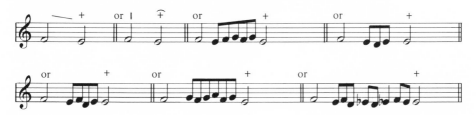

By *coulades* he means two or more notes moving conjunctly which fill in any
interval.[72]

Brossard notes that passages are best when sung on the vowels A, E, or O, rarely effective on I or Y, and forbidden on U.[73]

A distinction between articulated and slurred runs (*trait* and *coulade*) appears in
Montéclair's treatise. "The *trait* requires a single bow stroke, or a single articulation of the tongue on wind instruments for each note. The *coulade* sounds all

---

[69] *Ibid.*, xvii.
[70] *Ibid.*, xvii.
[71] Arger, *op. cit.*, 73.
[72] *Ibid.*, 74.
[73] Sébastien Brossard, in Arger, *op. cit.*, 74.

these notes on only one bow stroke, on one articulation of the tongue, or on the same syllable."[74]

The poems provided for French airs generally presented all their best poetic material in the first verse—maintaining the proper alignment between poetic and musical stress which was so important in French song. It was assumed, especially in seventeenth-century France, that a good singer would introduce copious passages in the second verse in order 1) to avoid the monotony of hearing a verse in which the words generally had little new to offer, and 2) to correct the defects in poetic accentuation which result from music which is composed specifically for the first, but not for the second verse.

Bénigne de Bacilly devotes a long chapter to passages and diminutions. He defends the principle of free embellishment, and recommends it not only for the second verse, but (sparingly and with taste) for the first verses "in order to pass easily from one note to the next."[75] It is impossible here to give more than a general summary and a couple examples to illustrate the manner in which Bacilly uses passages and diminutions to help the prosody of a second verse. The following examples are only the tip of Bacilly's iceberg.

There is a similar example a little further on in this same verse on the words 'en mourant,' in which the composer has joined the last syllable with the two preceding ones before making a *diminution* on it, even though in the first verse the last syllable of 'sommes' which is in the corresponding place is a whole tone away; that is, it descends to *mi*. The reason for this is that 'sommes' is feminine, and its next-to-last syllable is long; whereas, in 'mourant' the next-to-last syllable is short since the word is masculine and therefore the singer cannot stop on it. Thus, the singer must pass on to the last syllable by repeating the *fa* of the next-to-last syllable instead of performing it in its simple form as it appears on the word 'sommes.'

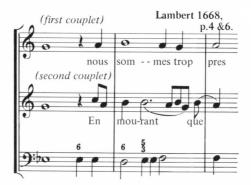

[74] Montéclair, *op. cit.*, xvii.
[75] Bacilly, *op. cit.*, 106 [212].

...there is another example of this re-aligment of syllables which are short in one couplet and long in the other. It appears on the words 'son humeur' where the composer has properly indicated that the first syllable of 'humeur' must be short since it is the next-to-last syllable of a masculine word; whereas, in the corresponding place in the first couplet, the first syllable of 'pensers' is long. This last statement may seem contradictory, since 'pensers' is also masculine. However, according to the rule regarding the 'n', this syllable must be seen as being long since the 'n' has the effect of making a long syllable out of an otherwise short one. ... The composer has taken consideration of this rule and has abstained from putting as many notes on this first syllable as would have been possible had the syllable been long, or at least has written the notes in a shortened fashion rather than in any other manner.[76]

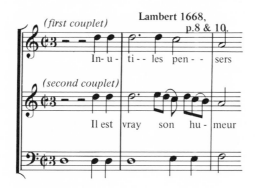

Bacilly advises a two-stage method for ornamenting second verses. First, one should make alterations which are suited to the long and short syllables of the text, by advancing or retarding the placement of the written notes. Second, one may add diminutions to whichever words would gain expressiveness through such embellishment, and which are deemed appropriate because of the length of their syllables.[77]

FOR THE ACCOMPANIST

In editing the *Fables* I have purposely omitted even a skeletal realization of the continuo, partly because the harmonies are so elementary that with a little practice one can improvise his own accompaniments. A simple four-part realization would be more misleading than informative. The following guidelines will be much more useful than the realizations which crop up in modern editions, and which are, in my opinion, nothing but an obstacle between the music and the accompanist.

1) Learn the words.

Le Coq et le Renard is not a story about chord progressions; the Rooster is not on guard against an invasion of parallel fifths. Text is the issue, and the accompanists's

---

[76] Bacilly, *op. cit.*, 108 [217]. The musical examples he quotes are by Michel Lambert.
[77] Bacilly, *op. cit.*, 110 [219].

first responsibility is to study the fable word-for-word. He should discuss the story and the pronunciation with the singer.

2) Sing the melody and the bass.

Let the ear be your guide. Begin by singing the melodic parts; the inner parts can join in later.

3) Look at the continuo symbols, and learn what harmonies are implied.

4) Experiment.

Go through the fable with the singer, discussing each section of the story. This is a "jam session" at which you use as wide a palette of color as possible in each section of the story. Retain what works. Throw out what doesn't. At this stage the following questions will guide you:

a) *Should the texture be thick or thin?* Dynamics at the harpsichord are largely controlled by texture. The sonatas of Domenico Scarlatti are the best example of dynamics controlled by texture, especially K. 208 in A major. Note how the left hand goes from five notes to one in making a resolution at the cadence point.

b) *Should the register be high or low?* Continuo playing should normally fall within the singer's range, but an occasional excursion into very high registers (for bird calls, etc.) as well as very low registers (for danger, or bears, etc.) only adds charm and variety to the music.

c) *Which sections are better suited by block chords? By broken chords?*

d) *How much dissonance should be included?* The *acciaccatura* is the accompanist's best friend. It fits in well with rolled chords and adds spice and accent to the harmony.

e) *Where should one play legato? Where staccato?* Remember that the latter has more energy than the former.

f) *How many registers (stops) should be used?* One may graduate from both hands on two "eights," to one hand on two "eights" and one on only one "eight," to both hands on only one "eight."

g) *Would a musette pattern help this fable*? Note that all the fables are marked *b.c. en musette*. The musette was a very popular bagpipe instrument, especially so in the eighteenth century when it had moved into courtly circles from its origin as a folk instrument. Undoubtedly the musette sometimes played along with the bass line in the fables. However, keyboard pieces sometimes imitated the musette, by using a drone pattern on *one* and *five* of the scale. This can serve nicely in the fables, as in *Le Renard et les Raisins* (see discussion of this fable on Page 34.)[78]

Introductions, Interludes, and Postludes

The *Fables* are rather bare as they stand — with neither an introduction to set the key, pulse, and mood, nor any interludes between the verses. Here the accompanist

---

[78] For examples of harpsichord pieces with a typical musette pattern, see "Muséte de Choisi" and "Muséte de Taverni," in François Couperin, *Pièces de Clavecin, Troisième Livre, Quinzième Ordre*, edited by Kenneth Gilbert (Paris: Heugel & Co., 1972) 38–41.

can be really creative by providing music which sets the stage — both textually and musically. In addition, this music can be the glue which turns a random bunch of fables into a cohesive 'set' for performance (assuming that one performs several fables in a group). Perhaps one fable will end with a few measures of harpsichord postlude, but the next one will begin with no introduction at all. Or another fable will end with no postlude, allowing the introduction of the next one to give the listener time to adjust to a new mood, and allowing the singer a little time as well.

Repeat Signs

The *Fables* are mostly in binary form, like most Baroque dances, with repeat signs in each half. The remainder are ternary ("Da Capo al fine"). The repeat signs need not be followed every time, especially in fables of many verses, where such repetitions would grow tiresome. Only take those repeats which stimulate your creativity by challenging you to vary and emphasize the performance. Sometimes the best solution is to repeat nothing except for the second half of the last verse — forming a *petite reprise*, as in *Le Coq et le Renard*.

SPECIFIC SUGGESTIONS DRAWN FROM
TWO PERFORMANCES OF THE FABLES

In March 1979, I had the pleasure of accompanying soprano Daureen Podenski, a student at the Juilliard School, in her Masters Recital. We performed songs from the Romantic and contemporary literature, along with five of the *Fables* (which we also performed at a Doctoral Seminar). Then in December of the same year, Carol Wilson, then assistant professor of voice at Carleton College in Minnesota, joined me in a recital at Carnegie Recital Hall.[79] There we presented another group of fables. I am greatly indebted to both artists for the care and perceptions they brought to these performances, from which the following discussion is drawn. Portions of these experiences are narrated here in the hope that they will enliven the resources of other performers, who will after all create new interpretations out of their own imaginations.

The first five fables discussed are from the performance at Carnegie Recital Hall; the last, *Le Paon*, is from Miss Podenski's recital at The Juilliard.

[79] "The rest of his program consisted of music by... plus six charming excerpts from the 'Nouvelles Poesies Spirituelles et Morales,' an 18th-century collection of short pieces from various sources. The first five of his selections were fables of La Fontaine set to tunes of the day. They were sung attractively — once she warmed up, which took one fable — by Carol Wilson, a soprano, and were helpfully accompanied by Mr. Metz." John Rockwell, review in *The New York Times* (Dec 23, 1979) 32.

La Fourmi, et la Sauterelle (Vol. I, Fable I)

See Chapter II, pages 13 and 14, for a comparison of several versions of this fable — from Aesop to the *Nouvelles Poésies*.

Miss Wilson and I felt that this fable should be introduced by music which imitated the laziness of summertime, so I improvised a rather legato introduction based on the second half of the musical setting. This contrasted with the jumpy playing I used for "Chante et bondit." On "l'oisiveté" we both turned to a more legato (lazy) approach. "Belle chanteuse, danse" offers a chance for real vocal contrast, and Miss Wilson gave her voice the appropriate tone of derision. We repeated only the second half of the last verse, as a *petite reprise*, and she added a *plainte* on the second syllable of "chanteuse" to heighten the harshness of the ant's reply.

Le Rat dans un fromage de Hollande (Vol. I, Fable IV)

Here the major interpretive goal was to make the most of the difference between the narrative of the first verse, and the direct moralizing of the second. A contrast in vocal color and articulation seemed to accomplish this. In addition we dotted the Da Capo of the second verse to make it more declamatory.

Le Renard et les Raisins (Vol. I, Fable XIX)

With any of the *Fables*, the harpsichordist has the option of a musette accompaniment, as the scores suggest (*b.c. en musette.*) We reserved the device for this, the most rustic tale in our set. I used the pattern in the example below as the musette. Two measures of the same music served as an introduction, and one measure as an interlude. The constant drone in the bass made the C sharp of the A-major chord unbearable to our ears, so I omitted that note from the harmony. This song allows the singer many subtleties of vocal color and facial expression, especially in the course of illustrating the Fox's voice.

La Lionne et l'Ourse (Vol. I, Fable XXI)

The repeated line of text which opens each verse of this tale calls for variety in color and dynamic. We chose to "echo" on verses one and four, but to reinforce the sound on verse two — in line with the quiet and passionate texts, respectively. In verse two I let my left hand "roar" like a lion, with lots of broken chords, dropping to only one or two notes at a time in verse four "Et l'Ourse dit tout bas: Tant pis, Madame." In this song the singer has ample opportunity to use varied colors, vibrato, and *son enflé* to illustrate a great range of emotion and action.

Le Coq et le Renard (Vol. I, Fable XXIII)

We had as much fun with this tale of barnyard wisdom as the fabled Rooster had in his victory over the cunning Fox. My introduction set up the Rooster's sentinel watch as follows:

There should be plenty of contrast within the first verse — from the Rooster's staccato strut to the Fox's legato wheedling. We felt that a brief interlude between each verse would help set up the following verse. Since the second and third verses each called for an accelerando, we used the interlude to bring the music back to the opening tempo before the next verse.

The laughter of verse four was characterized in the accompaniment by a more elaborate version of the introductory material, which I transformed into hen-like repeated notes in the style of Rameau's harpsichord piece, *La Poule.* I played this in the upper octave of the harpsicord in order to keep the accompaniment out of the singer's vocal range. Miss Wilson sang *sotto voce* at "On entend la poulaille..." so that when we repeated the second half of this verse (the only verse we repeated in this fable) it would really cackle with laughter.

Le Paon (Vol. IV, Fable VIII)

The Peacock is above all a song about singing, and is included here as an example of vocal ornamentation which was inspired by the text — as all good vocal ornamentation should be. Miss Podenski and I decided that no song needed to be set up more than this little tale of the Peacock and the Nightingale. I played through the song once on harpsichord, while Miss Podenski poised herself in a subtle but humorous way, which suggested the pose and haughtiness of the Peacock. It took some experimenting to find the suitable vocal color for the Peacock, for while this is a beautiful bird to see, its voice is as ugly as any common barnyard fowl. The Peacock's natural cry, "paon," is coarse in contrast to the Nightingale's lovely warble. So in the first verse Miss Podenski used a color which was not out of taste, but which was still as strident as she dared to make it. "Dit le Paon," was of course sung in a normal tone.

The second verse, in imitation of the Nightingale's beautiful voice, lends itself to ample ornamentation. What follows below is a mixture of the way Miss Podenski performed the second verse, along with some additional ornaments which she did not do. The result is very slightly exaggerated version which has the virtue (for study purposes) of including nearly all the ornaments discussed in Chapter III.

Verse I

Verse II, ornamented

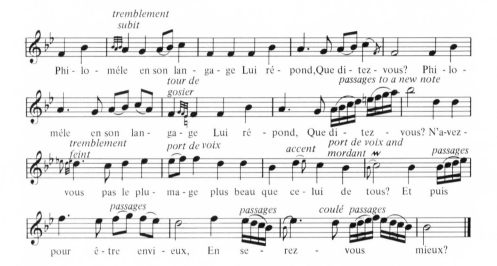

PART TWO

The Edition

IV.

Editor's Introduction

This edition is based on a microfilm prepared from a copy of the *Fables* in the Bibliothéque Nationale in Paris. In editing the *Fables* I have respected the original in every way possible, and at the same time I have attempted to provide a performable text. The original six-volume layout has been preserved; clefs have been modernized; but for reasons explained in the chapter on performance considerations, I have omitted any realization of the figures.

The original was generally clear enough that it could have been presented in facsimile, but several considerations induced me to rewrite the entire volume. There are places in the original where the word-engraving is not clear. Words are run together, and some letters are indistinct. The resulting questions of text were settled in the present edition by studying the context of the words, and by referring to complete and authoritative French dictionaries.

A majority of the airs originally appeared in soprano clef, and some of the bass parts were in tenor clef. While it is true that many musicians today read all the clefs with equal ease, there are those who would find a stumbling block therein. Since the *Fables* are meant to appeal to amateurs as well as to professional musicians, I felt that they should be presented in the familiar treble and bass clefs, in order to be as convenient today as they were in the eighteenth century. I notated the clef changes in the airs, but not in the accompaniments, where to do so would have interrupted the music. In addition, I completed the time signatures so that what read 3, for example, now reads $\frac{3}{4}$ or $\frac{3}{8}$. Key signatures were often incomplete, in accordance with eighteenth-century conventions. Thus G minor appeared with only one flat, and D minor with none. I added the accidentals to the signatures, and corrected the scores with naturals when the revised key signatures made this necessary. Also, where flats were cancelled with sharp signs, I used naturals instead. The bass figures were left pretty much as they were, except that I replaced the older x 6 with # 6 as the latter is easier to read.

The original edition was inconsistent in its manner of pointing out those fables which could be sung to more than one air. Notices appeared in a variety of places — next to the airs and at the bottom of pages (see p. 42). In addition, there are some fables which only fit airs from previous volumes. In order to straighten out the resulting confusion, I have provided an alphabetical index, which appears at the head of the Edition.

When I transcribed the songs, I purposely omitted one detail. The original scores had the first few words of text printed in small letters under the bass parts (see Appendix A, Plate 2, "Pendant l'été..."). This probably indicated that one could sing the bass line along with the solo part, as one of the many ways of performing the *Fables*.[80] I felt that the appearance of these words was distracting and unnecessary. One can still add a sung bass if desired.

As may be seen on **page** 124 , Plate 3, there were footnotes in the original edition. These served to explain various unfamiliar words thus: "Pinde" [a] "montagne fort haute." In the present edition these footnote letters have been replaced with asterisks.

Conclusion

The *Fables* from the *Nouvelles Poésies* resemble some of the programs on children's television, for, like "Sesame Street," La Fontaine set to music is both entertaining and sophisticated. *Le Fromage* (Vol.II, Fable V), for example, is similar to the confrontations between Bert and Ernie. In *Le Fromage* it is two Tomcats who lose their cheese to a Monkey whom they called upon to divide the cheese between them. Ernie of "Sesame Street" plays the same trick on Bert that the Monkey in the Fable played on the two Toms — namely he continues to eat the excess from each of two portions of cookies until they are all gone. There is also a similarity between the Road Runner cartoons and such Fables as *Le Coq & Le Renard* (Vol. I, Fable XXIII) or *Le Renard & le Loup* (Vol. I, Fable XI). In the *Fables*, as in the Road Runner cartoons, there is a message within the entertainment — "try to trick others, and you'll be tricked in turn."

Like children's television, the *Fables* are more than animated stories. They appeal to children on one level, and to adults on another. This dual nature may be musically analogous to the youthful simplicity of the vaudeville on one hand, and the mature sophistication of a Parisian salon on the other. It is only fitting, therefore, that a performance of the *Fables* should bring out both aspects. Indeed these songs will remain lifeless unless there are performers to animate them, and audiences to enjoy them. It is to such performers and audiences that I dedicate this edition.

---

[80] "One can also have the thoroughbass part sung, for which purposes I should then apply the text underneath, as well as it will go." Michael Praetorius, *Syntagma musicum, Tomas tertius (1619)*, Edited and translated by E. Bernouli (Leipzig, 1916). Quoted in Hermann Keller, *Thoroughbass Method* (New York: Norton, 1965) 32.

V.

The *Fables*

Facsimile of **Fable I**, Volume í (opposite).

VOLUME I

LA FOURMI, ET LA SAUTERELLE
Fable I (Sur l'Air,, "Qui l'entend mieux")
(L'Oisiveté)
English summary on p. 157

II

Pendant l'hiver,
La sauterelle est sans pitance;
Pendant l'hiver,
Elle est réduite à vivre d'air:

Et la Fourmi dans l'abondance,
Lui dit: belle chanteuse, danse,
Pendant l'hiver.

LE CORBEAU & LE RENARD
Fable II (Sur l'Air, "Pour passer doucement la vie.")
(La Flaterie)
English summary on p. 158

Vol. I/II e Air

Un Corbeau ten - ant   un   fro - ma - ge,   Au   haut d'un
arbre é - toit   per - ché;   Re - nard é - toit   au
voi - si - na - ge,   Et   par l'o - deur fut   al - lé - ché.

II	III
Le Rusé lui tint ce langage:	De plaisir l'oiseau noir croasse,
Peut-on voir plus gentil oiseau?	Le morceau lui tombe de bec.
Si la voix répond au plumage,	Le Renard vîte le ramasse,
Le monde n'a rien de plus beau.	Et dit: je vais souper avec.

IV

Apprenez poursuit-il, Beau Sire,
Qu'on ne vous flate point pour rien:
L'adulateur ne vous admire,
Que pour escroquer votre bien.

LE CONSEIL DES RATS
Fable III (sur le même Air)
(Le Grelot)
English summary on p. 158

I

Un Conseil dans une guérite
Fut tenu par le peuple Rat.
Tous dirent: pendons au plus vite
Une Sonnette au cou du Chat.

III

Qui va donc, dit enfin leur Doge,*
Au Matou mettre le Grelot?
Mais de tous ceux qu'il interroge,
Pas un ne lui répond un mot.

II

Nous sçaurons la marche et la route
Du Filou qui vient nous guetter.
C'etoit bien avise sans Doute;
Mais il falloit éxécuter.

Tout est plein, quand on délibere,
De courage et d'activité:
Mais pour agir, ce n'est plus guere
Que répugnance et lâcheté.

*Chef de la Republique

LE RAT DANS UN FROMAGE DE HOLLANDE
Fable IV (Sur l'Air, "L'etoit un petit l'Anche") (Noel Suisse)
(L'Hipocrite reclus)
English summary on p. 158

II

Je tiens tout hermite
Pour un hipocrite,
Si sa piété
N'a point de charité: (Fine)
Qu'on vante et public

Son austerité,
La misantropie
N'est point sainteté:
Que dans sa guérite
Il prie et médite;
(Je tiens tout hermite, etc.)

LE CHIEN QUI SE VOIT DANS L'EAU
Fable V (sur le même Air)
(L'Ombre pour le Corps)
English summary on p. 158

I

L'Onde transparante Au Chien
   représente
Le friand morceau Qu'il tenoit au
   museau (Fine)
Il quitte sa daube, Pour plonger
   dans l'eau:
Un autre la gobe: C'est là le
   plus beau:
Et le Berger chante D'une voix
   plaisante:
(L'Onde transparante, etc.)

II

Pour une espérance, Pour une
   apparance,
La cupidité Perd la realité.

C'est la maladie De l'humanité, (Fine)

Qui se sacrifice Pour la vanité:

En vain on la lance De son
   imprudence:
(Pour une espérance, etc.)

LE LOUP & L'AGNEAU
Fable VI (Sur l'Air, "Reveillez-vous")
(l'Oppression)
English summary on p. 158

Vol. I/IV Air
Léger et gracieux
Sur le cou - lant d'une on - de pu - re, Le Loup plus
haut, l'Ag- neau plus bas, Et -oient un jour par a - van -
tu - re Bien é - loig - nés de tren - te pas.
B.C. en musette

II	IV
(*fort*) D'abord le Loup commence à dire:	(*fort*) Si ce n'est toi, c'est donc ton frere,
Tu viens troubler l'eau que je boi.	Reprend le Loup sur le ton haut.
(*doux*) L'Agneau répond: Voyez Messire,	(*doux*) Comment cela se peut-il faire?
Qu'elle descend de vous à moi.	Je n'en ai point, répond l'Agneau.

III	V
(*fort*) L'an passé, dit la bête noire,	Mais, que lui sert de se
Contre moi tu t'es déchaîné.	deffendre?
(*doux*) L'Agneau répond: Comment	Dequoi lui sert la vérité?
le croire?	Il est mangé sans plus attendre,
Je n'étois pas encore né.	Comme s'il l'eut bien mérité.

VI
Plaignons le sort de l'innocence:
Elle reclame en vain les loix,
Quand l'injustice et la puissance
Contre elle s'arment à la fois.

LA GENISSE, LA CHÉVRE, LA BREBIS & LE LION
Fable VII (sur le même Air, de même que sur le deuxième Air)
(Le droit du plus fort)
English summary on p. 158

I

Avec les Grands ne t'associe,
C'est un avis des plus sensés;
Fui leur commerce, et t'en défie:
Tu ne sçaurois le craindre assez.

II

Un jour la Chévre et la Genisse
Chassoient avec le Roi des bois:
Mere Brebis quoi que nourrice,
Voulut aussi s'unir aux trois.

III

Le vain honneur toujours entraîne,
Et plus encor le vain espoir.
Qu'en revient-il? Bien de la peine,
Et puis c'est tout: nous l'allons voir.

IV

Un Cerf est pris: on le divise,
Comme il convient, en quatre lots:
Mais le Lion veut à sa guise
Toute la proie, et dit ces mots:

V

(Fiérement) Je suis Lion, et la
    premiere
Des quatre parts doit être à moi:
Et vous voyez que la derniere
Est un morceau bon pour le Roi.

VI

Pour le plus fort est la deuxiéme
Je la prens donc, car je le suis
Si quelqu'un touche à la troisiéme,
Il s'entira ce que je puis.

LES DEUX CHÉVRES
Fable VIII (Sur l'Air, "Dans notre Village")
(Le Point d'honneur)
English summary on p. 158

Vol. I/Ve Air

Léger

U - ne Chévre al - tiè - re sur un pe - tit pont,

B.C. en musette

Se trou - vra de front a - vec une au - tre non moins

fiè - re. Cé - dez - moi le pas: Il ne me plaît pas.

II
Dans cette dispute
Chévres s'agaçant,
Et s'entrepoussant,
Dans l'onde font la culebute.
Combien parmi nous
De semblables fous!

LA LICE & SA COMPAGNE
Fable IX (Sur l'Air, "Attendez-moi sous l'orne")
(L'Ingratitude)
English summary on p. 158

Vol. I/VIᵉ Air

Léger et marque

La Lice à sa voi-si-ne se fit prê-ter ja-

B.C. en musette   *grosse chienne

dis   Le lit et la chau-mi-ne, Pour fai-re ses pe-tits.

Huit jours, dit la com-me-re, Quinz au plus, c'est as-

sés: Mais ce fut une af-fai-re, Quand ils fu-rent pas-sés.

II	III	IV
Tonjours excuse prête	Mais quand la troupe forte	Ce qu'aux méchans on prête,
Pour ne point démarer:	Peut garder la maison,	N'est pas toujours rendu:
Requête sur requête,	On parle d'autre sorte,	En vain on le répète,
Aux fins de différer.	Sans rime ni raison.	Ce n'est qu'un soin perdu.
Attendez disoit-elle,	Inutile sermonce:	D'abord on vous amusé,
Que mes foibles enfans,	Mâtins restent dedans:	Bientôt il faut plaider:
Encore à la mamelle,	Et pour toute réponce,	Et la force, ou la rusé,
Soient devenus plus grands.	Montrent de bonnes dents.	Vous font enfin céder.

LA CHÉVRE, LE CHEVREAU & LE LOUP
Fable X (Sur l'Air, "Du cap de bonne esperance")
(La Méfiance)
English summary on p. 158-159

Vol. I/VIIe Air

II

Aussitôt qu'il voit la mere
A cent pas de la maison;
Ah! voici bien notre affaire,
Dit le cauteleux glouton.
Il ne court pas, mais il vole,
Et déguisant sa parole
Il s'approche du loquet,
Répétant le mot du guet.

III

Foin du Loup et de sa race,
Disoit-il entre ses dents.
Le Chevreau par la crevace
Lui répond: je vous entends;
Mais montrez mon patte blanche,
Ou bien attendez dimanche:
Patte blanche pour le coup,
Vaudra mieux que foin du Loup.

IV

Admirons la prévoïance
De la Bique dans ce fait,
Mais bien plus la méfiance
De notre petit Biquet.
L'avis de la bonne mere
N'auroit profité de guere,
Si le fils en animal
Ne peut pris qu'au littéral.

LE RENARD, & LE LOUP

Fable XI (Sur l'Air, "Si mon Ami vient en vendange")

(La Duppe)

English summary on p. 159

Vol. I/VIIIᵉ Air

Légèrement

Au fond d'un puits par a - van - tu - re. se lais -sa

B.C. en musette

cheoir Re - nard ma - tois.   On   ne va pas Tou - jours d'u - ne

dé - ma - rche   su - re,   Et Bu - cé - phale* a bron - ché quel - que fois.

*cheval d'Alexandre

II

Le prisoniere se prend à rire,
Et contrefaire le joyeux.
Le Loup vient, le regard: oh!
  Comment, mon bon sire,
Es-tu, dit-il, descendu dans ces
lieux?

III

Fort aisément, mon bon compere,
Répond Renard: fai comme moi:
Tu trouveras encor dequoi faire
  grand-chere,
Voi ce fromage; il est de bon alloi.

IV

Met dans ce seau ta corpulence:
Il se rencontre heureusement
Avec un autre ici qui le con-
  trebalance;
Et la voiture ira fort doucement.

V

Le sot entra dans la machine,
Et le rusé dans l'autre aussi.
L'un en bas, l'autre en haut en
  même tems chemine:
Et le rusé dit au sot, Grand merci.

VI

Mais qu'est-ce encor que ce
  fromage,
Qui du gourmand fut l'hameçon?
La Lune qui peignoit dans l'onde
  son image,
On nous séduit de semblable façon.

L'ANE PORTANT UNE IDOLE
Fable XII (Sur l'Air, "Nos plaisirs seront peu durables")
(Sot en dignité)
English summary on p. 159

1. Un Bau – det por – toit en vo – ya – ge Un faux
2. C'est ain – si qu'un soit s'i – ma – gi – ne, Que l'on

Dieu que l'on a – dor – oit: Et pour lui pre – noit tout l'hom –
rend à sa va – ni – té Les hon – neurs, que l'on ne de –

ma – ge, Qu'au Si – mu – laere on dé – fé – roit.
sti – ne Qu'à l'é – clat de sa dig – ni – té.

Vol. I/IXe Air
Léger
B.C. en musette

*Idole

LA MONTAGNE EN TRAVAIL
Fable XIII (sur le même Air)
(Grand bruit peu d'effect)
English summary on p. 159

I

Autre fois la vaste campagne
Frémissoit du mugissement,
Que poussoit certain Montagne
Dans un travail d'enfantement.

II

On croioit qu'une ville immense
Alloit naître après ces grand cris;
Mais le fruit de cette esperance
Fut, s'il vous plaît, une Souris.

III

Tous les jours le monde se vante
Et promet avec grand éclat:
Mais souvent tout ce qu'il enfante,
Ne vaut pas mieux que notre Rat.

L'ANTRE DU LION
Fable XIV (Sur l'Air, "J'ai perdu la liberté")
(La Prudence)
English summary on p. 159

Vers le Roi des a - ni - maux, Qui se di - soit ma-la - de,

Ceux des bois et des trou - peaux Al-loient en a - mbas-sa - de: Il nèst qu'un

seul des ses vas - saux, Que rien ne per - su - a - de.

II
On lui montre passeport,
Et toute autre assurance;
Le Renard tient toujours fort
Avec cette sentence:
Des ces beaux contes on endort
Les gens dans leur enfance.

III
Je vois que chez le Lion
De tous côtés on entre:
Cent chemin, dit-il y vont
Tout droit comme à leur centre;
Mais, dites-moi, comment fait-on,
Pour sortir de son antre?

LA PERDRIX & LE LEVRAUT
Fable XV (sur le même Air)
(Le Railleur puni)
English summary on p. 159

I
Gardez-vous bien d'insulter
Ceux qui sont dans la peine;
D'un génie à detester;
C'est la marque certaine:
Et j'entens dire et répéter;
C'est une ame inhumaine.

II
Mais sçavez-vous bien, qu'autant
Vous en pend à l'oreille?
S'il arrive à l'insultant
Avanture pareille.
Ah! voilà, dit-on, à l'instant,
Qui lui sied à merveille.

III
On raconte qu'un Levraut
Etant à l'agonie,
Et sous les dents de Miraut*
Prêt à laisser la vie;
La Perdrix crut dire un bon mot
Par cette raillerie.

IV
Vante-nous à l'avenir
Tes pieds et leur prouesse:
C'est Miraut qui sçait unir
La force à la vitesse:
Les liens pourront s'en souvenir,
S'ils ont de la sagesse.

V
Un Autour** qui l'entendit
Lui fit changer de note;
Comme un trait il descendit,
Et l'attrapa sans faute:
Et de par tout on entendit
Ces mots contre la sotte:

VI
Vante-nous à l'avenir
Ton aile et sa prouesse:
C'est l'Autour qui sçait unir
La force à la vitesse;
Les tiens pourront s'en souvenir,
S'ils ont de la sagesse.

*Chien de chasse
**Oiseau de proie

LE HÉRON
Fable XVI (Sur l'Air, "Quand je suis dans un repas")
(Le Dédaigneux)
English summary on p. 159

C'est la hon- te du *Hé- ron Que dans ces vers je chan- te. Qu'elle soit ou vraie, ou non, l'a- van- ture est tout de bon Plai- san- te, plai- san- te, plai- san- te.

*Oiseau aquatique qui vit de poisson

II	**III**
Tanche et Carpe sous ses yeux	Cependant tout ce poisson
En foule alloient se rendre;	Venant à disparoître,
Mais l'Oiseau tout dédaigneux	Dans sa faim notre Héron
Se disoit: Je ferai mieux	N'a qu'un fangeux limaçon,
D'attendre, d'attendre, d'attendre.	Pour paître, pour paître, pour paître.

IV
Tandis qu'il se lamentoit,
Triste et baissant la tête;
La Pie après lui chantoit,
Et sans cesse répétoit:
La bête! la bête! la bête!

LES DEUX MULETS

Fable XVII (Sur l'Air, "Ah! ma Commere es-tu fachée?")

(Faste dangereux)

English summary on p. 159

Vol. I/XIIe Air

Léger

Deux Mu-lets fais-oient un vo-ya-ge, L'un char-gé d'or,

B.C. en musette

L'aut-re de fruits de jar-di-na-ge, che-tif tré-sor.

Le pre-mier d'une al-lu-re fie-re, fai-sant le fat;

Lais-soit son com-pag-non der-rie-re, comme un gou-gat.

II

Au bruit qu'il fait de sa sonnette,
　　Vient le voleur:
On cherche l'or, et l'on se jette
　　Sur le porteur.
Il se deffend; mais on l'accable
　　De mille coups.
Gens fastueux, à cette fable
　　Que dites-vous?

III

L'autre Mulet que nul n'arrête,
　　Alloit son pas;
Et secoiiant un peu la tête,
　　Disoit tout bas:
J'estime fort, cher camarade,
　　Ton bel emploi;
Mais j'aime mieux porter salade;
　　Tu vois pourquoi.

LA GRENOUILLE & LE BOEUF
Fable XVIII (sur le même Air)
(L'Ambition)

English summary on p. 159-60

I

Chacun se tienne dans sa sphére
  Dit le bon sens.
Telle leçon est bonne à faire
  A bien des gens.
A qui n'en aime la pratique,
  Mal en prendra.
Ce fait risible, mais tragique
  Nous l'apprendra.

Une Grenouille ambitieuse,
  Pour égaler
Un Boeuf de taille monstrueuse,
  Voulue s'enfler.
Pleine de son project frivole,
  Elle s'enfla;
Et tant s'enfla la bête folle,
  Qu'elle en creva.

LE RENARD & LES RAISINS
Fable XIX (Sur l'Air, "Ton humeur est Catereine")
(Gasconade)

English summary on p. 160

Vol. I/XIIIᵉ Air

Un Re-nard dont le gé - ni - e sen -toit un peu le gas - con,

Et qui dans la Nor - man - di - e Au -roit pu donn - er le - çon;

Vit un jour sur un - e trel - le Grap- pe d'ex-cel -lent rai - sin,

Et dont la cou- lour ver-meil- le Per - met-toit re- pas très fin.

II

A sauter il s'évertuë:
Mais la proye etant trop haut,
Je servois, dit-il, bien gruë
D'essayer un autre saut.

Ce n'est que de la guenille,
Franc verjus pour des Goujats:
Qu'un autre à son gré le pille,
S'il lui plaît d'en faire cas.

LA BALETTE DANS LE GRENIER
Fable XX (Sur L'Air, "Quel Astre brille dans ce lieu?")
(Voleurs attrapés)

II

La Larronesse là dedans (bis)
Bon appétit et bonnes dents,
Sçut faire, sçut faire,
A l'aise et bien longtems
Très bonne chere.

III

Mais d'échaper C'est la le point (bis)
La bête creve d'un bon point
De sorte, de sorte
Que le trou ne peut point
Servir de porte.

IV

Dans les affaires d'un Seigneur, (bis)
Ainsi se glisse maint voleur
Pour prendre, pour prendre;
Et ne peut par malheur
Sortir sans rendre.

LA LIONNE & L'OURSE
Fable XXI (sur le même Air)
(Mal d'autrui n'est que songe)
English summary on p. 160

I

Dame Lionne avoit un fils, (bis)
Qui dans les rets un jour fut pris;
Vacarme, vacarme.
La Cour et la païs
Sont en allarme.

II

La Reine Mere rugissoit (bis)
Tant et tant, qu'elle étourdissoit
Le monde, le monde,
Des cris qu'elle poussoit
Loin à la ronde.

III

Tous les enfans, dit l'Ourse alors,
    (bis)
Qui sont tombés sous vos efforts
Naguere, naguere,
Pensez-vous qu'ils soient morts
Sans pere ou mere?

IV

Non repond l'autre; mais hélas,
    (bis)
Le mal d'autrui ne touche pas
Mon ame, mon ame:
Et l'Ourse dit tout bas:
Tant pis, Madame.

LE CERF SE MIRANT DANS L'EAU
Fable XXII (Sur l'Air, "Je fais souvent raisonner ma musette?")
(L'Utile & le Beau)
English summary on p. 160

Vol. I/XVe Air

Dans le cris - tal d'u - ne clai - re fon - tai - ne Un jeu - ne

B.C. en musette

Cerf se mi - roit au - tre - fois: Il ne voy - oit ses

jam - bes qu'a - vec pei - ne, Char - mé de voir la beau - té de son bois.

II

Soudain du cor entendant le
  murmure,
Promt et leger il fuit dans les
  forets;
Mais arrêté par sa belle ramure*

En expirant il pousse ces regrets:

III

Le beau nous plaît, et le bon
  nous ennuye:
L'un sert toujours, l'autre est
  souvent fatal.
Je méprisois ce qui sauvoit ma vie,
  vie,
J'amois, hélas! ce qui fait tout
  mon mal.

*Bois du Cerf

LE COQ & LE RENARD
Fable XXIII (Sur l'Air, "Boire à la Capucine")
(Fin contre fin)
English summary on p. 160

Vol. I/XVIᵉ Air

Léger

Un Coq en sen-ti-nel-le, veil-loit a-vant le

B.C. en musette

jour, Quand un Re-nard L'ap-pel-le, Pour lui jo-üer d'un tour:

Di-sant, la paix est fai-te, Et l'a-mi-tié par-fai-te: Tu

me vois dé-pu-té, Pour fai-re le trai-té

II	III	IV
L'Oiseau qui n'est pas bête,	La paix est générale,	Le Coq en rit, et chante
Répond, je suis à toi;	C'est ici le congrès.	A Poules et Chapons,
J'en jure par ma crête:	Mais le Renard détale,	L'aventure plaisante
Mais qu'est-ce que je voi?	Et gagne les guérets:	Qu'ici nous racontons:
Deux Chiens vers notre gîte,	J'ai, dit-il, une affaire,	On entend la poulaille
Accourent au plus vîte;	Je vais plutôt la faire;	Qui répete et criaille:
Et comme postillons,	Et je double le pas,	N'a pas petit honneur,
Franchissent les sillons,	Pour ne la manquer pas.	Qui trompe le tompeur.

LES OREILLES DU LIEVRE
Fable XXIV (Sur l'Air, "Car c'est une bouteille")
(La Peur)
English summary on p. 160

Vol. I/XVIIᵉ Air

II

Ah! dit-il, je suis banni,
J'ai deux cornes bien pareilles.
On lui dit en vain: nenni,
Ce ne sont que des oreilles.
Il répond toujours; détrompez-vous
Au gré des malins et des jaloux,
Oreilles seront cornes,
Voire cornes de Licornes.*

III

C'est ainsi, quand on a peur,
Que tout se métamorphose.
Un buisson est un voleur,
Un phantome ou pire chose.
Mais on sçait de même, qu'a la Cour
Un flateur fait prendre chaque jour
Les Merles pour Corneilles,
Et pour cornes les oreilles.

*Animal qu'a une grande corne sur le front

LE LION & L'ANE À LA CHASSE

Fable XXV (Sur l'Air, "O gué lan la")
(L'Air important)
English summary on p. 160-61

Vol. I/XVIIIᵉ Air

Un Li - on de Li - bi - e, Puis - sant chas - seur,
D'un Rous-sin d'Ar - ca - di - e fit son Pi - queur; Qui pous-
sant sa voix de *Sten - tor, Fit si bien le Cor, Et si bien son -
na, Que ce fut bou - che - rie Tout ce jour là.

*Soldat Grec qui avoit la Voix extremement forte.

II

De cette heureuse chasse
Le Clabaudeur,
De droit et non par grace,
Veut tout l'honneur:
Au Lion même il demandoit
Ce qu'il en pensoit.
Mais ce Sire là,
Avec une grimace
Le plante la.

III

Si par tout on condamne
L'air important
Qui souffriroit qu'un Ane
S'en Donnat tant?
Si chacun ne sçavoit tres bien,
Que les gens de rien
Sont comme cela:
Sans leur chercher chicane
Laissons les là.

LES MEMBRES & L'ESTOMAC
Fable XXVI (sur le même Air)
(La Mesintelligence)
English summary on p. 161

I

Les Membres conspirerent
Abhoc, abhac:
Et tout net déclarerent
A l'Estomac,
Qu'ils étoient las de tant veiller,
De tant travailler
Pour ce Monsieur là:
Et puis il persisterent
Sur ce pied-là.

II

De la mutinerie
Quel est le fruit?
L'humeur qui vivifie
Bientôt s'enfuit.
Tout est triste, foible et perdus,
Le sang ne va plus
Deçà, ni delà:
Jugez quelle est leur vie
Sur ce pied-là.

III

Par cette experience
Chacun revient:
Et dans l'intelligence
Tout se maintint
Désormais, plus de mécontens,
Ni de fainéans:
Tout se n'habilla.
Heureux l'Etat qui danse
Sur ce pied-là.

VOLUME TWO

L'HIRONDELLE, ET LES PETITS OISEAUX
Fable I (Sur l'Air, "Je vous ai donné, etc.")
(L'Indocilité)
English summary on p. 161

Vol. II/Ier Air
Gai et gracieux

Vous qui voy - ez naî - tre ce lin, Di - soit u - ne Hi - ron - del - le, Ar - ra -chez, sans lais - ser un brin, De cet - te herb mor - tel - le: Pour vous pren - dre pe - tits Ois - seaux, D'el - le se font laqs et ré - seaux.

B.C. en musette

II	III	IV
Alors les uns de sommeiller,	Oisillons en foule attrapés,	Vous préchez inutilement
Ou rire à leur maniere,	Gisent dans la cuisine.	A qui ne veut entendre:
Et les autres de babiller	Si l'on fait grace aux plus hupés,	Mais il arrive fréquemment,
Contre la Conseiller.	En cage on les confine;	Comme au tems de
Mais tout ce qu'elle avoit prédit	Où fredonnant couci couci,	Cassandre,*
Arriva, comme elle avoit dit.	On nous dit qu'ils chantoient ceci	Que l'auditeur vient à sentir
		Un inutile repetir.

*Fille de Priam, qui prédit la prise de Troie

L'OURS, ET LES DEUX GASCONS

Fable II (Sur l'Air, "Je n'air pour toute maison")

(La peau de l'Ours)

English summary on p. 161

Vol. II/IIe Air

Marqué

Deux Gas - cons man-quoient d'ar - gent, Et s'a - vi - se - rent

B.C. en musette

d'al - ler ven - dre La peau d'un Ours am - bu - lant, Qu'ils s'en - ga - ge - rent

d'al - ler pren - dre. En moins de deux ou de trois

jours, Ils de - voient é - cor - cher leur Ours: Mais ce - lui-

ci de son co - té, Se mo-qua de ce beau trai - té.

II

Cependant ils vont tous deux,
Et s'en promettent la conquête,
L'Ours parut, et les cheveux
   Se hérisserent sur leur tête.
L'un, plus habile s'échapa,
Au plus haut d'un chêne grimpa.
L'autre, à courir un peu moins fort,
Se couchant, contrefit le mort.

III

Autour de l'homme gisant,
Qui point ne bouge et ne respire,
   Notre bête alloit flairant,
   Et se grimace sembloit dire:
   Il faudra rompre le marché;
   Point de peau, j'en suis bien
     faché.
   Quand vous voudrez la mattre à
     prix
   Attendez que vous m'ayez pris.

LE CHÈVRE, LE MOUTON, ET LE COCHON GRAS
Fable III (sur l'Air précédent)
(Plaintes inutiles)
English summary on p. 161

I

Dame Chévre et dom Mouton
Alloient ensemble, dit l'histoire.
Avec eux un gras Cochon
Etoit encore de la foire.
Ils n'alloient pas pour filouter,
Ni pour voir Tabarin sauter.

On sçait bien que ces beaux
  desseins
Ne sont faits que par les humains.

II

Loin de rire, le Pourceau
Soupire et pleure à sa maniere.
On diroit que du couteau
Il voit la lame meurtriere.
Les deux autres ne disoient rien,
Et je crois qu'ils faisoient fort
  bien:
Quand le mal ne peut s'éviter,

A quoi sert de se lamenter?

LE RENARD, ET LE BOUC
Fable IV (Sur l'Air du premier Recueil) (See page 50)
(La Prévoiance)
English summary on p. 161

I

Avec un Bouc peu sage,
Mais bien haut encorné,
Jadis faisoit voyage
Renard le rafiné:
La soif vient à les prendre:
Un puits se trouve après:
Et nos gens d'y descendre.
Comment sortir après?

II

Voici ce qu'il faut faire,
Dit le Renard matois.
Lève tes pieds, compére,
Et dresse bien ton bois:
Le long de ton échine
En haut je grimperai;
Puis par quelque machine,
Je te reguinderai.

III

Par ma barbe touffue,
Dit son sot compagnon,
Jamais ne fut conçue
Plus belle invention.
Cependant l'autre monte,
Il sort du mauvais pas,
Et laisse plein de honte
Messire Bouc en bas.

IV

Puis il fait à la bête
Cet important sermon:
Plus de sens dans la tête,
Moins de barbe au menton.
C'étoit lui faire entendre,
S'il eut été plus fin,
Qu'avant que d'entreprendre,
Il faut prévoir la fin.

LE FROMAGE

Fable V (sur l'Air, "Tiquetique et lon lan la")

(Fureur de plaider)

English summary on p. 161

II

Il faut, dit-il, aux deux Gars,
Bien égaliser les parts.
Qu'on m'apporte une balance:
Dans chaque bassin mettons un lot.
Ce trait de jurisprudence
Dans le Code* est mot pour mot.

III

Voyons, puisque c'est à moi
De juger selon la loi.
Cette part est trop pesante,
Poursuit-il, et croque l'exédent:
L'autre ensuite prend la pente;
C'est un autre coup de dent.

IV

Coups de dent de plus en plus,
Tant qu'il reste de surplus.
Enfin presque rien ne baisse:
Bon, disent alors les Contendans.
Sans que Maître Bertrand cesse
D'exercer encor ses dents.

V

Pour l'exacte égalité,
Dit-il avec gravité
L'equilibre est necessaire:
Ceci branle encor; il faut rogner.
Croyez-vous qu'en telle affaire
Je sois juge à m'épargner?

VI

Il fait si bel et si bien,
Qu'il ne laisse presque rien;
Et ce peu qui reste encore,
Pour le droit d'épice est réservé.
Le Magot donc le dévore:
Le fromage est achevé.

VII

Nos Matous s'en vont maltés:
On en rit de tous cotés.
Cependant, quoi qu'on en die,
L'on ne sçauroit vivre sans procès.
Ni guérir de la manie
De manger son bien en frais.

*Recueil des Lois

LE GEAI, PARÉ DES PLUMES DU PAON

Fable VI (Sur l'Air, "Le Printems rappelle aux armes")

(Vanité ridicule)

English summary on p. 161-62

II

A chacun son personnage,
   Nous dit le Sage,
A chacun son personnage
   Sied toujours bien.
A sortir de son étage
L'imprudent ne gagne rien.

III

Témoin le Geai misérable.
   Que peint la fable,
Témoin le Geai misérable
   Parmi les Paons:
Aux Paons vil et méprisable,
Odieux à ses parens.

IV

Il s'étoit mis dans la tête,
   La pauvre bête!
Il s'étoit mis dans la tête
   Qu'il brilleroit;
Prenant la plume et la crête
D'un beau Paon, lorqu'il mueroit.

V

Il le fait avec parade,
   Puis se panade,
Il le fait avec parade,
   Et s'applaudit
Mais le Paon, quoi que malade,
Lui fit bien changer d'habit

VI

Il accourt avec sa bande
   Nombreuse et grande,
Il accourt avec sa bande,
   Sur notre Oiseau:
Coups de bec vont de commande,
Et le plument bien et beau.

VII

Il s'enfuit vers sa famille,
   Tout en guenille:
Il s'enfuit vers sa famille,
   Qui le hua:
Et tout jusqu'au moindre drille,
De lardons le salua.

LE RAT, ET L'HUÎTRE
Fable VII (sur l'Air, "Tarare ponpon")
(Le Badaut)
English summary on p. 162

Vol. II/Vᵉ Air

Un Rat qui n'a voit fait que vinqt pas à la ron- de, Au-tour de son lo-

B.C. en musette

gis, trop voi- sin du ma- tou; Rat qui n'a- voit vu l'on- de Ja-

mais ni peu ni prou, Quit- ta, pour voir le mon- de, son trou.

II	IV

La mer n'étoit pas loin: le faiseur
  de voyage
Aprés peu de chemin, s'y trouva
  transporté;
  Et vit sur le rivage
  Nombreuse quantité
  De menu coquillage
  Resté.
	Mais le plus beau du jeu, c'est
	  une Huître qui baille,
	Quand le Soleil commence à
	  darder ses rayons.
	  C'est quelque victuaille,
	  Dit le Sot, approchons:
	  Allons, vaille que vaille,
	  Mangeons.

III	V

De vaisseau de haut bord c'est une
  flotte immĕnse,
Aux yeux de l'innocent, qui ne
  sçait ce que c'est;
  De même sorte il pense
  Sur tout nouvel objet.
  Tel est de l'ignorance
  L'effet.
	Plein de bon appétit (Rats en
	  ont à revendre)
	Dans l'écaille entr'ouverte
	  il s'allonge et s'étend,
	  L'Huître pour se deffendre,
	  Se referme à l'instant.
	  Ainsi tel qui croit prendre,
	  Se prend.

LE MEUNIER, SON FILS, ET L'ANE
Fable VIII (sur l'Air précédent)
(On ne peut plaire à tous)
English summary on p. 162

I
Un Meunier et son Fils, gens
  d'illustre mémoire,
Portoient comme un ballot,
  leur Baudet suspendu;
   Afin, nous fait-on croire,
   Qu'étant frais et dodu,
   Il fut mieux a la foire
   Vendu.

II
Le premier qui les vit, eut
  bien là dequoi rire,
Et dequoi plaisanter sur le
  couple idiot:
   Aussi sçut-il leur dire
   Leur fait, bien comme il faut,
   Et faire leur satire
   Tout haut.

III
Le Meunier l'entendit; et
  sentant sa bêtise,
Détacha la Bourique, et
  la fit détaler:
   Mais un autre s'avise
   Bientôt de contrôler;
   Chacun veut à sa guise
   Parler.

IV
L'Ane est pour vous porter,
  leur dit-il, Qu'il nous porte
Répondirent nos gens, méttant
  l'Ane sous eux.
   Un censeur d'autre sorte
   Leur dit d'un ton hargneux,
   La Bęte est trop peu forte
   Pour deux.

V
Le Pere descendit, non
  l'Enfant, Quelle honte!
S'ecrie un vieux Bourgeois:
  hola! ho! mal appris!
   Que le Vieillard remonte:
   Vous, descendez, beau fils,
   Fussiez vous Baron, Comte,
   Marquis.

VI
Le Pere remonté, quelques
  Drilles passerent,
Et ne voulurent point voir
  à pied le garçon:
   Au Vieillard insulterent
   De la belle façon,
   Et cent fois l'appellerent
   Barbon.

VII
Glosera qui voudra, dit-il
  presqu'en colere:
Je ne consulterai que moi
  seul désormais;
   Vouloir à tous complaire
   C'est être bien niais.
   Quand pourra-t'on le faire?
   Jamais,

L'HOMME, LA CITROUILLE, ET LE GLAND
Fable IX (Sur l'Air, "Je suis charme")
(La Providence)
English summary on p. 162

Vol. II/VIe Air
Légèrement

Ad - mi - rez la Pro - vi - den - ce, Trou - vez bon ce

B.C. en musette

qui lui plaît, Dans le plus pro - fond si - len - ce

Ré - vé - rez ce qu'elle a fait; Et cor - ri - gez

vo - tre im-pru - den - ce, Et cor - ri - gez vos pré - ju - gez.

II	**III**
Cette tige est trop menue	Et ce Gland, qu'a-t'il à faire
Pour la Gourde*que voila:	D'un grand mât pour son appui?
Il falloit l'avoir pendue	S'il s'en tient au nécessaire,
A l'un de ces chenes là.	On ozier suffit pour lui:
C'eut été mieux	C'est ce que dit
A notre vue,	Un téméraire,
C'eut été mieux,	C'est ce que dit
Disent nos yeux.	Un sot esprit

*Espece de Calebace moins grosse qu'une Citrouille

IV

Mais tandis que notre bête
S'occupe de tels propos,
Le Gland tombe sur sa tête
D'un des arbres les plus hauts.
  Le raisonneur
  Alors s'arrête,
  Le raisonneur
  N'est plus censeur.

V

Laissons, dit-il, à leur place
La Citrouille avec le Gland.
Qu'auroit fait la Calebace
De se haut, dégringolant?
  J'étois brisé
  Sous cette masse,
  J'etois brisé,
  Pulvérisé.

LE RENARD, ET LE BUSTE
Fable X
(sur l'Air précédente)
(Vaine apparence)
English summary on p. 162

I

On nous dit qu'au tems antique
Un Fondeur en bronze creux,
Exposa dans sa boutique
Le Portrait d'un certain Preux*
  Chacun crioit
  Au magnifique.
  Chacun crioit,
  Et l'admiroit.

II

Le Renard vient, et se mêle
Dans l'amas de ces Badants
Oui, dit-il, la tête est belle,
Mais elle a de grande deffaut.
  Je n'en dis qu'un,
  Point de cervelle;
  Je n'en dis qu'un
  Assez commun.

*Guerrier

LE STATUAIRE
Fable XI (Sur l'Air, "Dirai-je mon confiteor")
(L'Illusion)
English summary on p. 162

II

Son art sçait exprimer si bien
L'air d'une foudroyante Idole,
Qu'on trouve qu'il ne manque rien
A son Jupin* que la parole.
Même l'on dit que l'Ouvrier
S'en effraya tout le premier.

III

Chacun tourne en réalités
Autant qu'il peut, ses
    propres songes.
On est de glace aux vérités
Et tout de feu pour les mensonges.
L'esprit sans cesse en est séduit,
Et par malheur le coeur le suit.

*Jupiter

L'HUÎTRE, ET LES PLAIDEURS
Fable XII (Sur l'Air, "Que j'estime mon cher voisin")
(Le Procès)
English summary on p. 162

Vol. II/VIIIe Air

Un jour, di-sent nos Chro ni-queurs, N'im-porte en quel cha-pi - tre;

B.C. en musette

Che-min fai - sant, deux Vo - ya -geurs Ren-con- trerent u - ne Huî - tre.

II En pareil cas il faut plaider, C'est le train ordinaire: Et l'on voit, sans le demander, Ce que devint l'affaire.	**III** Le fond paroît être fort bon A Maître Dandin, Juge, Qui pour loyer de son jargon, Ouvre l'Huître, et la gruge.

IV
Telle est la fin, pauvre Plaideur,
De tes longues batailles.
Laisse ton Huître au Sénateur,
Emporte les écailles.

LE RAT, ET L'ELÉPHANT
Fable XIII (Sur le même Air)
(Sotte Vanité)
English summary on p. 162

I Un Rat auprès d'un Eléphant De corpulence énorme, Disoit: Un Rat vaut bien autant Dans sa petite forme.	**III** Tandis qu'il fait le triomphant, Un Chat vient, qui s'en moque: Un Rat n'est pas un Eléphant, Dit-il, et puis le croque.
II Qu'importe qu'on occupe ici Ou plus ou moins d'espace; Je n'en tien gueres, mais aussi J'ai beaucoup plus de grace.	**IV** Ce Rat, qui dans sa vanité Se crut un personage, De l'humaine fatuité Sera toujours l'image.

L'ANE, VÊTU DE LA PEAU DU LION
Fable XIV (Sur l'Air, "Les Fanatiques que je crains")
(Le Fanfaron)
English summary on p. 162-63

Vol. II/IXe Air

Légèrement

1. L'A - ne sous la peau du Li - on, se ren- doit re - dou - ta - ble;
2. Plus d'un se don - ne pour Hé - ros; Et dans son vain lan - ga - ge,

B.C. en musette

Mais si - tôt qu'on sçut son nom, La Bê - te mé - pri - sa - ble, Ne pa - rut
Fait bien haut son - ner les mots De force et de cou-ra - ge; Mais a - près

qu'un fan - far - on Qu'un A - ne vé - ri - ta - ble.
ces beaux pro - pos, Nôtre Ane est son i - ma - ge.

LE RAT DE VILLE, ET LE RAT DES CHAMPS
Fable XV (sur le même Air)
(La vie champêtre)
English summary on p. 163

I

Le Rat de ville au Rat des champs
Un soir faisoit grand' chere:
Mais un triste contretems
Gâta toute l'affaire:
Du logis viennent les gens;
Les Chats ne tardent guere.

II

Adieu, dit le Rat villageois
Au Citadin tout blême;
Jamais au fond de nos bois
Je ne tremblai de même:
Je vous laisse avec vos Rois
Et votre peur extrême.

LA TORTUE, ET LES DEUX CANARDS
Fable XVI (Sur l'Air, "Assez longtems j'ai menagé")
(Babil imprudent, et vaine Curiosité)
English summary on p. 163

Vol. II/Xe Air

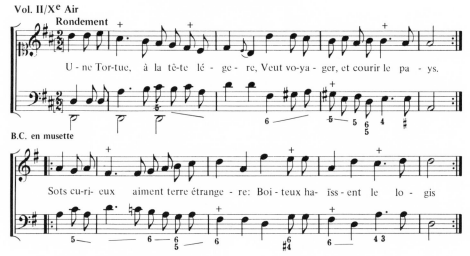

Rondement

U - ne Tor-tue, à la tê-te lé - ge - re, Veut vo-ya - ger, et courir le pa - ys.

B.C. en musette

Sots cu-ri- eux aiment terre étrange - re: Boi - teux ha - ïss - ent le lo - gis

II
Par deux Canards est faite une machine.
Cette machine étoit un long bâton,
Ou par les dents tenoit la Pélerine:
Serrez bien ferme, lui dit-on.

III
Les deux Oiseaux la portent par les nues:
Tout s'ébahit, et l'on crie en tous lieux:
Ah! venez voir la Reine des Tortues
Dans le chemin qui mene aux cieux.

IV
Oui, Je la suis, Messieurs, ne vous déplaise,
Dit l'innocente, et lâche le bâton:
La Dame tombe; on rit de sa fadaise:
Mais elle en pleure tout de bon.

LES POISSONS, ET LE CORMORAN
Fable XVII (sur le même Air)
(Sotte Confiance)
English summary on p. 163

I
Qui penseroit que le peuple
    aquatique
Se fut laissé dupper au Cormoran;*
En transportant toute sa république
Dans le vivier de ce Tiran?

II
Ce fut l'effet d'une terreur panique
Que l'Oiseau sçut, dit-on, leur
    inspirer:
Le Pecheur vient, leur dit le
    Politique;
Venez chez moi vous retirer.

III
Quand il les tient enfin sous sa
    puissance,
Le protecteur se met à les croquer:
S'associer, donner sa confiance
A tels mangeurs, c'est se moquer.

IV
Que le Poisson est une sotte
    engeance!
On nous en fait cent contes
    differens.
Mais les humains sont encore, je
    pense,
En cas pareils plus sottes gens.

*Gras Oiseau qui se nourrit de Poisson

LE PÊCHEUR, ET LE PETIT POISSON

Fable XVIII (Sur l'Air, "Vous qui vous moquez par vos ris")

(Profiter du présent)

English summary on p. 163

Vol. II/XIᵉ Air

Légèrement

Pe - tit Poisson de - viendra grand, Si Dieu lui prê - te vi - e;

Mais le la - cher en at - ten - dant, Je tiens que c'est fo - li - e, Je me con-

ten - te du pré - sent. C'est ma phi - lo - so - phi - e.

II

Ainsi parloit d'un Carpillon
Un Pêcheur assez sage,
De qui j'appris cette leçon,

Ou plutôt cet adage*:
Vant mieux au sac petit Goujon,
Que gros Brochet qui nage.

*Proverb

LA JEUNE DOGUE, ET SA MERE
Fable XIX (sur le même Air)
(Perte utile)
English summary on p. 163

I

Tel crie, et va se lamentant,
Qui ne me touche guére:
C'est l'orsqu'il perd, et qu'en perdant
Il fait très bonne affaire.
Tâchons dans le récit suivant
D'expliquer ce mistere.

II

Un Dogue, né pour le troupeau,
Où pour choses pareilles,
Voyant tomber sous le couteau
Ses deux grandes oreilles,
Disoit: Vraiment je serai beau!
On m'acoutre à merveilles.

III

Pourquoi de plus ce gorgerin
Ou cette énorme fraise:
Cet accablant colier d'airain,
Qui trente livres pése?
Me l'a-t'on fait faire à dessein
De me mettre à mon aise?

IV

Ma Mere, vous ne hurlez pas,
Loursqu'ainsi l'on m'outrage:
En si piteux et triste cas,
Vous faites bon visage.
Mais, quoi! vous souriez, hélas!
Quand je creve et j'enrage.

V

Va va, ce n'est que pour ton bien,
Répond la bonne vieille.
Afin que tu ne risques rien,
Ainsi l'on t'apareille.
Contre les Loups il faut au Chien
Carcan et point d'oreille.

LE RENARD, ET LE CHAT
Fable XX (sur l'Air Ier du premier Recueil) (see page 1)
(Les Expediens)
English summary on p. 163

I

Maître Renard
S'applaudissoit de sa finesse,
Maître Renard
Disoit à maître Rodillard:
Sans faire tort à ton espèce,
Nul Chat n'égale en fait d'adresse
Maître Renard.

II

J'ai mille tours,
Que j'ai déja mis en usage.
J'ai mille tours,
Et j'en invente tous les jours.
Soit dans les bois, soit au village:
Pour me sauver de tout domage,
J'ai mille tours.

III

Maître Matou
Dit: J'en sçais un, et m'en contente,
Maître Matou
Dit: J'en sçais un, et j'en ai prou.
Seul il répond a mon attente:
Change de ton, Compere, et vante
Maître Matou.

IV

Je sçais grimper,
Quand le Basset* de pres me chasse,
Je sçais grimper
Pour l'empêcher de m'attraper.
Lorsque toujours chageant de place,
Pour le tromper, Renard se lasse,
Je sçais grimper.

*Chien de chasse

V

Tes mille tours
Souvent te tirent mal d'affaire,
Tes mille tours
Plus d'une fois se trouvent courts,
Et c'est en quoi le mien differe;
N'attends pas que je lui préfere
Tes mille tours.

VI

N'en ayons qu'un;
Et s'il est bon, qu'il nous suffise:
N'en ayons qu'un:
Le trop grand nombre est importun.
Renard est fin; mais quoi qu'il dise,
Matou dit mieux. C'est ma devise.
N'en ayons qu'un.

L'ANE, ET LE PETIT CHIEN

Fable XXI (sur l'Air IIe du premier Recueil) (see page 44)
(Le Lourdaut)
English summary on p. 163

I

Un Baudet disoit en son ame,
Voyez donc ce Toutou mignon,
Avec Monsieur avec Madame
Il est de pair à compagnon.

II

Que fait-il? il donne la pate,
Et d'abord il est courtisé.
Imitons-le, pour qu'on nous flate;
Cela n'est pas si mal-aisé.

III

Ainsi dit: il porte à la joue
De son Maître amoureusement,
Un large pied couvert de boue,
Et son chant fait le compliment.

IV

O la charmante mélodie!
O le beau jeu! dit le Patron.
Mais pour finir la comédie,
Faisons danser martin baton.

V

Un lourdaut, jamais, quoi qu'il
    fasse,
Ne sera qu'un mauvais plaisant.
Vous ne ferez rien avec grace,
Si vous forcez votre talent.

LE LOUVAT, ET LE CHEVAL

Fable XXII (sur l'Air Ve du premire Recueil) (see page 49)
(L'Indiscretion)
English summary on p. 163

I

Un Louvat* novice
Qui n'avoit rien vu,
Ilanté, ni connu
Que les enfans de sa nourice,
Trouva sur ses pas
Un Roi de haras**

II

Il lui dit: Beau Sire,
Quel est votre nom?
L'autre lui répond:
Tu le sçauras, si tu sçais lire:
On l'a copié
Autour de mon pié.

III

Le Nigaud s'approche,
Lorgnant de son mieux.
Entre les deux yeux
Messer Cheval vous lui décoche
Un coup bien serré,
De son pied ferré.

IV

Puis la pétarade,
Pour le divertir,
Ou pour l'avertir
D'aller chercher son camarade
Parmi les Louvais,
Et loin des haras.

*Jeune Loup
**Beau Cheval

L'AIGLE, ET LE CORBEAU
Fable XXIII (sur l'Air XVI du premier Recueil) (see page 62)
(Exemple dangereux)
English summary on p. 164

I
L'Example est une amorce.
Qui trompe bien des gens
Sans génie et sans force,
Imitateurs des Grands.
On sue, on se tourmente;
Et le projet qu'on tende,
Souvent a pour tout fruit
La honte qui le suit.

II
Un Aigle est toujours Aigle,
Corbeau n'est que Corbeau;
Mais cette sage regle
Déplaît au noir oiseau:
Il veut se satisfaire,
Faire ce qu'il voit faire
Au Pere de l'Aiglon,
Qui vole le Mouton.

III
Après bien de la peine,
Et bien du tems perdu;
Ses deux pieds dans la laine
Sont pris comme à la glu:
Mais tandis qu'il s'empêtre,
Il voit venir le Maître
Qui le prend bel et bien,
Et le donne à son chien.

LA POULE AUX OEUFS D'OR
Fable XXIV (sur l'Air XVIIᵉ du premier Recueil) (see page 63)
(L'Avidité)
English summary on p. 164

I
Une Poule qui pondoit
Un Oeuf d'or chaque journée,
A son Maître répondoit
D'un trésor pour chaque année:
Mais par un caprice impertinent
Il voulut avoir incontinent
En main toute la somme,
Et se crut un habile homme.

II
Ce n'etoit qu'un idiot,
Et le plus sot de la foule,
En disant: J'ai le gros lot
Dans la panse de ma Poule:
Il la prit soudain et l'éventra,
Et pas un brin d'or n'y rencontra;
On la mit au potage,
Pondit-elle davantage?

VOLUME THREE

LA BESACE
Fable I
(L'Amour Propre)
English summary on p. 164

Vol. III/Ier Air

Branle de Metz - Légèrement

Cha - cun a ses a - van - ta - ges, Et cha - cun a ses dé -

B.C. en musette

fauts: Mais par - mi les a - ni - maux. Dom - es - ti - ques et sau -

va - ges, Cha - cun croit ê - tre le mieux, Et vou - droit tous les ho -

ma - ges: Cha - cun croit ê - tre le mieux, Et lui seul plait à ses yeux.

II	III
Jadis dans leur assemblée,	L'Ours très content de sa forme
(Car jadis il s'en faisoit)	Fit la moue à l'Eléphant,
Le Magot* s'applaudissoit	Disant qu'il étoit trop grand,
De sa tête bien moulée;	Et sa masse trop informe.
Et sur l'Ours, qu'il honnissoit,	L'Eléphant de son côté
Faisoit faire la huée:	Ne veut point qu'on le réforme:
Et sur l'Ours, qu'il honnisoit,	L'Eléphant de son côté
Comme un Arlequin glosoit:	Dit mainte autre pauvreté.

*Le Singe

IV	V
Monstrueuse est la Baleine;	Nous portons tous la Besace
La Fourmi n'est qu'un fêtu:	Qu'Amour Propre nous donna.
N'est-ce-pas? qu'en penses-tu?	Tout Mortel arrange là
Dit-il à l'espece humaine.**	Les defauts de chaque classe:
Celle-ci mépris a tout,	Par devant sont ceux d'autrui,
Se donnant louange pleine:	Et les siens à l'autre place:
Celle-ci mépris a tout,	Par-devant sont ceux d'autrui,
Seule parfaite à son goût.	Et les siens derriere lui.

**L'Homme

L'ANE, ET LE CHIEN
Fable II (Sur l'Air, "Heureuse l'enfance")
(Secours mutuel)
English summary on p. 163

II	III	IV
On dit que la Bête**	Trop loin de son Maître	Pour ne point se rendre
Qui mange chardons	Qui s'est endormi,	De quoi sert l'effort
Au prix de sa tête	Etant allé paître	Comment se défendre?
Brava ces leçons;	Il voit l'ennemi,	Le Loup est trop fort:
Au Chien son confrere	Le Loup sanguinaire,	Il prend, il déchire
Qui mouroit de faim,	Qui vient á grands pas:	L'Ane sans tarder,
N'ayant daigné faire	Mais l'Ane a beau braire,	Et le force à dire:
Part d'un peu de pain.	Le Chien ne vient pas.	Il faut s'entre-aider.

*L'Ane

LE SINGE ADOPTÉ
Fable III (sur le même Air)
(Le Naturel)
English summary on p. 164

I

De la gent Magote
Sottement épris,
Un Homme à marote
N'ayant point de fils.
Se mit dans la tête
D'adopter Bertrand,*
Et fit de la bête
Son unique enfant.

II

Voila Monsieur Singe
Paré richement:
Beau drap, et beau linge.
Plus beau diamant,
Peruque bien blonde,
Plumet au chapeau
Annoncent au monde
L'Adonis nouveau.

III

Il a Pédagogues
De toutes façons,
Sçavans dialogues,
Sçavantes leçons.
On est à lui faire
Prendre tous les plis,
Qu'un millionaire
Fait prendre à son fils.

IV

Enfin avec l'âge
On devient majeur:
Bertrand hors de page
Et sans gouverneur
Dérange, cheffonne,
Grimpe sur les toits,
Magot en personne
Tout comme autrefois.

V

Que sert la tournure,
Et l'air, et l'habit?
Jamais la Nature
Ne se contredit.
La métamorphose
Du tempérament,
N'est pas une chose
Qu'on fasse aisément.

*Singe

LE SATIRE, ET SON HÔTE
Fable IV (Sur l'Air, "Le fameux Diogene")
(La Duplicité)
English summary on p. 164

Vol. III/IIIe Air
Légèrement

O - yez un bon Sa - ti - re: L'on ne sçau - roit mieux

B.C. en musette

di - re Que cet Ours mal-lé - chés: Son mot est d'un vrai

Sa - ge: En faut- il da-van - ta-ge? E - so - pe l'a pré - ché.

II

Or voici l'anecdote:
A table il voit son Hôte
Souffler diverses fois,
Tantôt sur ce qu'il touche
Pour porter á sa bouche,
Et tantôt sur ses doigts.

III

Pourquoi cela Compere?
L'autre explique l'affaire
En bon Phisicien:
Mais le Silvain sur l'heure
Le fait de sa demeure
Déguerpir bel et bien.

IV

Va dit-il, je te prie
Souffler en Normandie:aire
Le mieux c'est le plûôt:
Loin des lieux où je couche;
Qui souffle de sa bouche
Et le froid et le chaud.

L'ASTROLOGUE, QUI SE LAISSE TOMBER DANS UN PUITS

Fable V (Sur l'Air de la Pastorelle de Monsieur Couperin)
(Vanité de l'Astrologie)
English summary on p. 164-65

Tel fait l'ha - bile en ho - ro - sco - pe Et pré - tend li - re dans les cieux, Tan-dis quil cho - pe Com-me une Tau - pe, Et sous son nez ne voit pas mieux: Le bon E - so - pe Nous dé-ve - lo - pe Là des-sus un fait mer - veil - leux.

II

Avec une longue lunette
Longnoit un de ces Sçavantas,
Pendant qu'il guette
    Quelque planette,
Un puits se trouve sur ses pas
    Le faux Prophete
    Soudain se jette
Au fond du creux qu'il ne voit
    pas.

III

Mai cependant, quoi qu'on en
    die,
Femmelettes et bonnes gens
    Ont la folie
    Et la manie
De consulter ces charlatans.
    L'Astrologie
    Et la magie
Auront encore des chalans.

LE LIÉVRE, ET LES GRENOUILLES
Fable VI (sur le même Air)
(Le Poltron)
English summary on p. 165

I
Ah! s'écrioit un Liévre au
      gîte,
Ah! que la peur rend
      malheureux!
   Un rien agite,
   Et dans la fuite
Se sauve á peine le Peureux.
   Mais fuyons vîte:
   De ma guérite
J'entends sonner un cor ou
      deux.

II
C'étoit pourtant bruit de
      zéphire:
Et l'animal voit son erreur.
   Mais sans mot dire,
   Aux champs il tire,
Et sur ses pas croit le chasseur.
   On a beau lire,
   Voir, et s'instruire,
On ne guérit point de la peur.

III
Notre Poltron dans son voyage
Trouve Poltrons plus grands en
      encor
   A son passage
   Un marécage:
Offre Grenouilles sur son bord:
   La gent sauvage
   Vite à la nage
Vers son azile prend l'essor.

IV
Eh! quoi! l'on fuit, lorsque je passe,
Dit le coureur. Qu'est donc ceci?
   Prenons de grace
   Un peu d'audace:
Mais il faudroit du coeur aussi:
   Et notre race,
   Quoi qu'elle fasse,
N'aura jamais qu'un coeur transi.

LA VIEILLE, ET LES DEUX SERVANTES
Fable VI (Sur l'Air, "Ah! ma Commerce es-tu fâchée?")
(De mal en pis)
English summary on p. 165

Vol. III/Vᵉ Air
Gaiment

Chez u - ne vieil - le   deux Ser - van - tes E - toit, dit - on:

B.C. en musette

Et tou - tes   deux   très   mal con - ten - tes, Non sans rai - son:

Tou-jours fi - ler,   tou - jours   en   cham - bre Leur è - toit   hoc,

Et se le - ver,   même   en   dé - cem - bre, Au   chant du   Coq.

II

Ah! maudit Coq, se dirent-elles,
   Tu périras:
Plus de la voix ni de tes aîles
   N'éveilleras:
Sous le couteau bientôt expire
   L'Oiseau fâcheux:
Mais tout alla de mal en pire,
   Loin d'aller mieux.

III

Tout la nuit dans sa demeure
   La Vieille au guet,
Tracasse et demande à toute
   heure
   Quelle heure il est:
On ferme encor moin les paupieres
   Qu'auparavant:
Mieux étoient donc nos filan-
   dieres
Le Coq vivant.

LES DEUX CHIENS

Fable VIII [No inscription in original]
(L'Inclination)
English summary on p. 165

Vol. III/VIe Air

Marqué

De deux Chiens fré-res et ju - meaux Chan-tons l'hi - stoi- re: De deux Chiens fré-res et ju -

B.C. en musette

meaux Nés tout é - gaux. L'un se fit aux grands tra - vaux, Domp-ta mil-le Le-

vrauts, Et se couv-rit de gloi - re, Ho - no - ré pour cet é - gard Du beau nom de Cé - sar.

II	**III**
L'autre fut un vrai fainéant,	Parmi nous, voire chez les Rois,
Chien de cuisine:	C'est tout de même:
L'autre fut un vrai fainéant,	Parmi nous, voire chez les Rois,
Sot et gourmand,	Souventes fois
Bien mangeant et bien dormant:	De deux fréres que j'y vois,
Ce fut tout son talent,	L'un par de beaux exploits
Et toute sa routine:	Acquiert honneur suprême;
Pour cela le marmiton	L'autre à rien ne paroit bon,
Le nomma Laridon.	Et n'est qu'un Laridon.

LE SINGE, ET LE LÉOPARD
Fable IX (Sur l'Air précédent)
(La Variété)
English summary on p. 165

I

Gille Singe avec Léopard
 Moins fin que Gille,
Gille Singe avec Léopard
 Chacun à part,
Avoient affiché placard;
 L'un pour montrer son art
 Aux Badauts de la ville,
Et l'autre étaler aux yeux
Son habit curieux.

II

Léopard dit: Venez, Messieurs,
 Voir un miracle:
Léopard dit: Venez Messieurs.
 Voir mes couleurs:
Nul parterre avec ses fleurs,
 Ne peut former ailleurs
 Un bigaré spectacle,
Comme la variété
De mon poil marqueté.

III

Gille dit: Je promets des jeux
 De toute espece
Gille dit: Je promets des jeux
 Selon vos voeux:
Cent et cent sauts périlleux,
 Cent tours ingénieux,
 Cent mille de souplesse
Et cette variéte
N'a jamais dégouté.

IV

Le Matois connoissoit les gens
 Et la nature
Le Matois connoissoit les gens,
 Tels de tous tems.
On court après les brillans
 Et les traits différens
 Qui font la bigarure;
Mais on l'aime dans l'esprit,
Bien plus que sur l'habit.

LE SAVETIER ENRICHI
Fable X (Sur l'Air, "Si mon ami vient en vendange")
(Inquiétude des richesses)
English summary on p. 165

II

Dès lors il craint qu'on ne le
vole
Il est aux champs au moindre
bruit,
Autour de son trésor sans
cesse, il caracole,
Et ne dort plus ni le jour ni la
nuit.

III

L'argent n'est point béatitude:
Croire autrement, c'est une erreur.
Qui cherche à s'enrichir, cherche l'inquiétude,
Et s'enrichit souvent pour son
malheur.

LE LOUP PLAIDANT CONTRE LE RENARD, PAR DEVANT LE SINGE

Fable XI (Sur l'Air, "Bel Astre que j'adore")
(Jugement du Singe) (Noel de M. Pélégrin)
English summary on p. 165

Vol. III/VIIIe Air

Légèrement

Du Sin - ge de la fa - ble Chan - tons le ju - ge - ment.

B.C. en musette

Son ar - rêt é - qui - ta - ble Fut fait sub - ti - le - ment.

D'a - bord la vrai sem - blan - ce Le con - tre - dit:

Mais si - tôt qu'on y pen - se, L'on ap - plau - dit.

II	III	IV
Un loup mis en justice	Le Juge de sa place	Payez tous deux l'amende,
Par le Renard rusé,	Jettant les yeux sur eux,	Nonobstant tout appel;
Sans preuve et sans indice	Leur dit: Méchante race,	Et puis que l'on vous pende
D'un vol fut accusé:	Je vous connois tous deux:	A chacun un cartel!
Il se deffend, et nie	Renard, quoi qu'il en die,	L'un de noire machine
Qu'il ait rien pris,	N'a rien perdu;	Sera notté,
Et sur la calomnie	Et Loup de volerie	Et l'autre de rapine
Fait les hauts cris.	Est convaincu.	Etiqueté.

LES DEUX VOLEURS, ET L'ANE
Fable XII (Sur le même Air)
(Pêcheur en eau troublé)
English summary on p. 165

I

Par deux Frippons à pendre
Un Ane fut volé:
Chacun vouloit le prendre
De là grand démêlé
C'étoit querelle vive,
Et tout de bon
Pour la finir arrive
Un tiers Larron.

II

Sur la Bourique il monte,
Et pique bel et bien:
Les autres à leur honte
Se sont battus pour rien.
Mieux fait qui s'accommode,
Sans s'arrêter
A la bisare mode
De contester.

LE PAÏSAN, ET L'OURS
Fable XIII (Sur l'Air, "Que j'estime, mon cher voisin" — Air II du IIe
Recueil) (see page 68)
(Le Sot officieux)
English summary on p. 165

I

Ne faites point société
Avec ami sauvage:
Craignez même de sa bonté
Votre plus grand dommage.

II

Un Homme eut, dit-on autrefois
Un Ours pour compagnie:
C'est ce qu'on trouve dans les bois:
Prudent qui s'en défie.

III

Sous le nez de l'homme endormi
Se jouait une mouche,
Et d'un pavé son sot ami
L'écrasa sur sa bouche:

IV

Il avoit bonne intention;
Mais c'étoit une bête,
Qui crut servir son compagnon,
Et lui cassa la tête.

VOLUME FOUR
LE COMBAT DES BÉLETTES, ET DES RATS
Fable I (Sur l'Air, "Ah! qu'il est beau l'oiseau!")
(Faste dangereux)

English summary on p. 166

II
Mais les Bélettes, et les Rats
(bis)
Ce sont les Chefs et les Soldats
Que j'aime, que j'aime
A suivre sur leurs pas
Dans mon poëme.

III
Je vois déja leurs bataillons,
(bis)
Qui couvrent les vastes sillons:
La rage, la rage
Est peinte sur leurs fronts.
Ah! quelle image!

IV
Mais on se mêle, et tout d'un tems,
(bis)
Tombent milliers de combatans:
La plaine, la plaine
De morts et de mourans
Est toute pleine.

V
Le Peuple Rat plie et s'enfuit,
(bis)
Sa soldatesque en maint réduit
Se cache, se cache:
Mais plus d'un Chef périt
Par son panache.

VI
Ils avoient mis pour leurs signaux,
(bis)
Casques cornus, avec faisceaux
D'aigrette, d'aigrette:
De là vinrent leurs maux
Dans leur retraite.

VII
Nul trou n'est assez spacieux
(bis)
Pour leur ouvrir à quelque creux
Passage, passage:
Et l'ennemi fait d'eux
Un grand carnage.

VIII

Le faste n'est qu'un peu de vent:
   (bis)
Mais ce vent cause bien souvent
   L'orage, l'orage,
Qui précipite un grand
   Dans le naufrage.

LA BÉLETTE, ET LE LAPIN

Fable II (Sur l'Air, "La Liberté préside")
(Chatte-mitte)
English summary on p. 166

II

Dans cette incertitude
Pour arbitre fut pris,
Parmi la multitude,
Maître Mange-souris.*

III

Faisant la Chatte-mitte,
Le sourd, le maupiteux,
Près de lui l'hipocrite
Les fait venir tous deux.

IV

Il faut, dit l'Escogrife,
Finir vos différens;
Et d'une double griffe,
Les happe en même tems.

V

Aux donneurs d'audience
Je porte grand respect:
Mais je fuis leur présence;
Chez eux tout m'est suspect.

VI

Sur tout le doux langage
D'un vieux Maître filou,
Dont le patelinage
Imite le Matou.

*Chat

LE CHAT, ET LE VIEUX RAT
Fable III (sur le même Air)
(La Précaution)
English summary on p. 166

I

Invention nouvelle
Pour attraper souris
On en tient le modéle
D'un Raminagrobis.*

II

En haut la Bête fine
Se suspend par un pié:
Chacun croit à sa mine
Voir un supplicié.**

III

Souris dans leur guérite
Ne se renferment plus:
Le pendu résuscite,
Et leur saute dessus.

IV

Nous en sçavons bien d'autres,
Leur dit le Papelard;
Vous serez toutes nôtres
Ou plus-tôt ou plus-tard.

V

Qu'est-ce qu'il imagine
Pour en venir à bout?
Il prend de la farine
Et s'en fait un surtout.

VI

Dans une huche ouverte
Il va donc se fourer:
Et les Rats pour leur perte
Vont à l'entour flairer.

VII

Mais un vieux Rat devine
La ruse du filou:
Ce n'est son ni farine,
Dit-il: C'est un Matou.

VIII

Au moins je le soupçonne:
Croyez-moi mes amis:
La méfiance est bonne
Pour n'être point surpris.

*Chat
**Pendu

L'ENFANT, ET LE MAÎTRE D'ÉCOLE
Fable IV (Sur l'Air, "Expert en pilotage")
(Le Pédant)
English summary on p. 166

Ha - ran - gue sur ha - ran -gue, Que sert tant de dis - cours? Pé - dant, bri - de ta lan-gue, Et vien à mon se - cours: Vien vîte et me re - lé - ve, Di - soit un jeune E- lé - ve Prêt à pé - rir dans l'eau; Lors- que son Pé da - go - gue Lui fai - soit d'un ton ro-gue Ser- mon tou-jours nou veau. .

LE POT DE TERRE, ET LE POT DE FER
Fable V (sur le même Air)
(La Témérité)
English summary on p. 166

Aux risques de l'orage
Pourquoi vous exposer?
Si vous faites naufrage,
Qui peut vous excuser?

Une Cruche d'argile
A se briser facile,
Au Bronze se heurtoit;
Quand elle fut cassée,
On dit de l'insensée,
Qu'elle le méritoit.

LE LION, ET LE MOUCHERON
Fable VI (Sur l'Air, "Ma raison s'en va bon train")
(L'Arrogance)
English summary on p. 166

Vol. IV/IVᵉ Air
Gaiment

B.C. en musette

Tres sou - vent pe - ti - tes gens Sont ter - ri - bles aux plus grands.

grands Un vil mou-cher - on Har - céte un Li - on, Et le met hors d'a - lei - ne, A-vec un si min - ce ai-guil - lon, Qu'on ne le voit qu'à pei - ne Lan - la Qu'on ne le voit qu'à pei - ne. Un ne.

II

Mais le Sire avoit grand tort,	L'Insecte volatile:
Et chacun le blame fort,	Ah! le voila récompensé
D'avoir agacé	De sa morgue incivile,
Grondé, menacé	Lanla, De sa morgue incivile.

LE LION, ET LE RAT
Fable VII (sur le même Air)
(L'Humanité)
English summary on p. 167

I	II
Un Rat se trouva, dit-on	Quelque peu de jours après
Sous les pattes d'un Lion.	Le Lion fut pris aux rets:
Le fier Animal,	Alors notre Rat
Sans lui faire mal,	Ne fut point ingrat,
Loin d'entrer en furie	Ni de petit usage:
Avec tendresse lui parla,	Il accourut vite et rongea
Et lui donna la vie,	Les cordons de la cage,
Lanla,	Lanla,
Et lui donna la vie.	Les cordons de la cage.

III

Très souvent petites gens
Sont utiles aux plus grands:
Mais je dis aussi,
Qu'il faut que ceux-ci
Soient bons et charitables,
Et ne me disent point: Voila
Propos de vieilles fables.
  Lanla,
Propos de vieilles fables.

LE PAON ET LE ROSSIGNOL

Fable VIII (Sur l'Air, "Ce charmant vin de Champagne")

(L'Envie)

English summary on p. 167

II

Philoméle en son langage

Lui répond, Que dites-vous?

N'avez-vous pas le plumage

Plus beau que celui de tous?

Et puis pour être envieux

En serez-vous mieux?

LE RENARD, ET LE LION
Fable IX (sur le même Air)
(L'Accoutumance)
English summary on p. 167

I
Un Renard par avanture
Tomba chez le Roi des bois;
Et n'ayant vu sa figure
Jusques là que cette fois,
Il en fut saisi d'horreur,
  Et pama de peur.

II
Le Lion, bonne personne,
(Chose rare dans un Grand)
Dit aux Pages: Qu'on lui donne
Au plutôt un restaurant;
Et s'il est remis ce soir,
  Je veux le revoir.

III
Le soir donc on le raméne:
Il paroît devant le Roi.
Dans cette seconde scéne
L'Acteur craint, mais sans effroi.
Qu'il revienne encor demain,
  Dit le Souverain.

IV
Selon l'ordre on le présente,
Quand le Prince sort du lit,
Et qu'avec sa Cour riante
Gravement il cause et rit.
Le Renard en est charmé
  Loin d'être allarmé.

V
Peu s'en faut qu'il ne s'oublie
Et ne soit trop familier.
Avec le Monarque il lie
Entretien particulier.
Les vieux Courtisans jaloux
  S'émerveillent tous.

VI
A la longue accoutumance
Céde la difficulté.
Crainte, haine, répugnance.
Tout par elle est surmonte.
Mais on va par son moyen
  Au mal comme au bien.

LA COUR DE LION

Fable X (Sur l'Air. "Un sot qui veut faire l'habile")
(Le Fin Courtisan)
English summary on p. 167

Vol. IV/VIᵉ Air

Sul-tan Li-on vou-lant con-noi-tre De quels su-jets il é-toit sou-ve-rain, De-vant lui les fit com-pa-roî-tre Et son pa-lais un jour en é-toit plein; Lors-qu'a l'en-droit où le Mo-nar-que dî-ne,L'Ours bou-cha sa na-ri-ne C'é-toit une o-deur; Un fu-met dont la va-peur Lui sal-sit le coeur.

II	III
Le Roi lui fit dans sa colere	Mais le Renard plus fin s'en tire,
Sentir qu'il faut être moins dégouté.	Disant, J'ai pris un rhume par
Le Singe approuva cette affaire,	malheur.
Vanta l'odeur et la sévérité.	Quand le Roi veut lui faire dire
Il s'y prit mal, sa sotte flaterie	Ce qu'il avoit jugé de la senteur.
De même fut panie;	De tout ceci facilement j'infere
Lion lui parla	Que qui ne veut déplaire,
Comme un vrai Caligula*	N'est ni trop flateur,
Et puis l'étrangla.	Ni trop sincere parleur
	Avec un Seigneur.

*Empereur cruel

LA MOUCHE, ET LE COCHE
Fable XI (sur l'Air précédent)
(Vain empressement)
English summary on p. 167

I

Dans un amas d'epaisse boue,
Etoit un Char bien-avant engagés
L'essieu plongeoit avec la roue,
Et le Charton crioit en enragé:
Quand là-dessus une Mouche
  s'approchez
Faisons aller ce Coche,
Dit-elle en venant,
Voltigeant, allant, tournant,
Toujours bourdonnant.

II

Ces chevaux là sont des masettes,
Poursuivit-elle, et de son aiguillon
Piquoit plus vif que des molettes*
Tantot au flanc et tantot au chignon:
Elle parloit en mal de l'attelage,
Pour faire davantage
Priser son beau soin
Et montrer qu'elle est à point
Venue au besoin.

III

Enfin on se tire d'affaires
L'impertinente enpretent tout
  l'honneur;
Elle veut encor un salaire
Argent comptant pour son fameux
  labeur.
O qu'il en est de cette espece vaine
Parmi la ràce humaine!
Gens à s'empresser,
Gens à nous embarasser,
Gens bons à chasser.

*Eperon

L'AIGLE, LA CORNELILLE, ET LA TORTUE
Fable XII (Sur l'Air, "Quand le péril est agréable")
(Conseil scélerat)

English summary on p. 167

Vol. IV/VIIe Air
Légèrement

L'Aigle a-voit   pris   u - ne Tor - tu - e,   Et ne son - geoit

B.C. en musette

qu'à   la   man - ger;   Mais elle é - toit   hors   de   dan -

ger   D'é - cail-les   re - vê - tu - e.

II

Quoi que le Sire s'evertue,
Son bec de fer ne perce point;
La Dame en rit dans son pour-
   point
D'écailles revêtue.

III

Une Corneille malotrue
Vint dire à l'Aigle sur cela,
Que peut le bec sur celle-là
D'écailles revêtue?

IV

L'ecornifleuse continue:
Promettez-m'en un bon lopin;
Et vous verrez qu'elle est en vain
D'écailles revêtue.

V

A moitié t'en est dévolue,
Respond l'oiseau qui s'ennuyoit
De voir la viande qu'il tenoit,
D'écailles revêtue.

VI

Lâchez dit l'autre, de la nue
Sur un rocher solide et sec
La belle qui résiste au bec
D'écailles revêtue.

VII

Sur le roc tombe la Tortue,
Son toit se brise en se heurtant;
Sa chair n'est plus dès cet
   instant
D'écailles revêtue.

VIII

La force moins souvent nous tue
Que les conseils d'un
    Scélérat.
Souvenous-nous en tout combat,
De la pauvre Tortue.

LE MULET ENTÊTÉ DE SA NOBLESSE
Fable XIII (Sur l'Air, "Adieu paniers, etc.")
(A quelque chose malheur est bon)
English summary on p. 167-68

II	III
Il dédaignoit d'être au service	Devenu vieux on le confine
Des Médecins les plus huppez	Avec les Anes au moulin;
Et leur disoit: Vous vous trompez	Son Pere lui revint enfin
Si vous croyez qu'on vous obéïsse.	Qui comme lui portoit la farine.

IV

On dit fort bien, qu'à quelque chose
Assez souvent malheur est bon.
Il met un fat à la raison
D'un bon effet il est donc la cause.

LE LION S'EN ALLANT EN GUERRE
Fable XIV (sur le même Air)
(Tout sert en ménage)
English summary on p. 168

I
Sire Lion, pour une guerre
Fit avertir les Animaux
Et leur manda par ses
   Prèvôts
De s'assembler de toute la terre.

II
Pour voiturer le nécessaire
L'Elephant doit prêter son dos,
L'Ours s'apprêter pour les
   assauts,
Et le Renard pour ce qu'il sçait
   faire.

III
Il rusera par sa finesse:
Et d'espion nous servira;
Le Singe encor amusera
Les ennemis par ses tours
   d'adresse.

IV
Mais l'Ane, lourde et sotte race,
Ne peut, dit-on, de rien servir.
Le Lièvre aussi, qu'un rien fait
   fuir,
Que voulez-vous Sire, qu'on en
   fasse?

V
Le Roi répond, qu'on les
   admette.
Je sçaurai bien les employer.
Le Lièvre agile est bon courier
Et l'Ane est bon pour être
   trompette.

VI
Les Souverain prudent et
   sage
Discerne et place les talens.
Entire les mains d'habiles gens
Rien n'est oisif, Tout sert en
   ménage.

LE CHÊNE, ET LE ROSEAU
Fable XV (Sur l'Air, "J'ai foison de dettes et de procès")
(Plier à propos)
English summary on p. 168

Vol. IV/IXe Air
Gaiment

Je te plains, dit le Chêne au Ro - seau,   On te   voit   flé - chir

B.C. en musette

sous   un moi - neau.   Pour - ras   tu sou-te - nir la   tem - pê - te?

Tu tom-be - ras à son pre mier ef - fort: Mais quel   poids pour-roit

char - ger   ma tê - te - ?   Et con-tre   moi quel vent   est   as - sez   fort?

<table>
<tr><td>

II

Nous verrons, dit l'Arbuste
  aussitôt,
Qui sçaura s'en tirer comme il
  faut.
A l'instant l'Aquilon en furie
Abbat le Chêne avec un grand
  fracas:
Le Roseau sans résistance plie,
Et sort ainsi de ce triste
  embarras.

</td><td>

III

Ce récit vous laisse à deviner
S'il est bon toujours de
  s'obstiner,
Ou s'il faut, quand le danger
  vous presse,
Sçavoir céder à la
  nécessité.
Vain effort n'est jamais que
  foiblesse:
Courage seul n'est que
  témérité.

</td></tr>
</table>

L'ANE CHARGÉ DE SEL, ET L'ANE CHARGÉ D'ÉPONGES
Fable XVI (sur le même Air)
(Imitation dangereuse)
English summary on p. 168

I

Deux Baudets trouvant sur leur
  chemin
Un fossé profond et d'eau bien plein,
Le Premier heureux par avanture
Avec succès dans l'onde
  s'élança.
Tout le sel, qui faisoit sa voiture
Fondit bientôt, et le porteur
  passa.

II

Le Second croyant que sans
  danger
Il alloit aussi se soulager,
Sans tarder comme l'autre se
  plonge.
L'autre fit bien, celui-ci fit fort
  mal:
Il portoit un gros paquet
  d'éponge.
Même chemin pour tous n'est
  pas égal.

LE LOUP BERGER
Fable XVII (Sur l'Air, "N'oubliez pas, etc.")
(Trompeur pris dans son piége)
English summary on p. 168

Qui veut trom-per, sou-vent s'a-bu-se: La ru-se Dé-
ce-le le trom-peur. Si bien que fas-se
l'im-pos-teur Par quelque en droit son jeu l'ac-cu-se.

B.C. en musette

II

Témoin ce Loup, dont on nous conte
  La honte
Et le destin fatal.(fin)
On veut parler: on parle mal,
Et la machine se démonte
Témoin ce Loup etc.

III

En hoqueton ou souquenille
  Le Drille
Se fit voir au troupeau. (fin)
Contre la tige d'un armeau
Se tenant droit comme une quille.
En hoqueton etc.

IV

Il prétendoit ainsi surprendre,
  Et prendre
Bon nombre de Brebis. (fin)
C'est pour cela qu'il avoit mis
L'acoutrement qu'on vient d'entendre.
Il pretendoit etc.

V

Le Sot voulut comme Titire*
  Leur dire,
Au pain, Moutons, au pain. (fin)
Sachant déja de longue main
Que c'est le mot qui les attire.
Le Sot etc.

*le Berger

VI

Il n'eut pas mal joué son rôle,
  Le Drole,
On l'eut pris pour Berger. (fin)
S'il avoit sçu mieux ménager
L'air et le ton de la parole.
Il n'eut etc.

VII

Mais à sa voix, voix de furie,
  Tout crie,
A la bête, au larron. (fin)
Sous les habits de Coridon
Il faisoit bien la comédie.
Mais à etc.

VIII

Et le vilain, quand on le brave,
  S'entrave
Dans l'habit emprunté. (fin)
Jusqu'au Mouton le plus crotté,
Pour l'assomer tout fait le brave.
Et le etc.

L'ARAIGNÉE ET LA GOUTE
Fable XVIII (sur l'Air précédent)
(Chacun à sa place)
English summary on p. 168

I

L'Aragne un jour dit à la Goute
  Ecoute,
Je quitte mon logis. (fin)
Quoi que ce fut doré lambris
Marbre éclatant superbe voute.
  L'Aragne etc.

II

L'on me tracasse et l'on me
  presse
  Sans cesse
A grands coups de balais.(fin)
Dequoi me sert un beau Palais
Où je ne trouve que tristesse?
  L'on me etc.

III

Depuis un an que dans ce gîte
  J'habite.
Je n'eus un bon moment. (fin)
Je l'abandonne incessament
Et je déménage au plus vîte.
  Depuis etc.

IV

Si tu le veux, vien sans attendre
  Le prendre,
Et me donne le tien. (fin)
L'autre répond, je le veux bien:
Dans le mien tu n'as qu'à
  descendre.
  Si tu etc.

V

La Goute étoit chez un pauvre
  homme
  Tout comme
L'on est au Châtelet. (fin)
Dans un manoir obscur et laid
Et pour vous dire tout en
  somme.
  La Goute etc.

VI

Malgré la differance étrange
  L'echange
Fit leur commun bonheur. (fin)
La Goute est mieux chez un
  Seigneur,
L'Aragne est mieux dans une
  grange.
  Malgré etc.

LE CIERGE
Fable XIX (Sur l'Air, "Le fameux Diogene" — Air III du IIIᵉ Recueil) (see p 87)
(L'Ignorance)
English summary on p. 168

I
Sachez votre Logique
Avec votre Physique
Autant que vous pourez.
Mais, pourquoi je vous prie
Tant de Philosophie?
Un mot: vous le verrez.

II
Un Cierge à ce qu'on chante,
(La chose est fort plaisante)
Croyoit duroir au feu,
Voyant par la pratique
Qu'ainsi faisoit la brique
Il en savoit bien peu.

III
Par ce trait d'ignorance
Dans la flame il s'élance:
Il y fond à l'instant.
Voyant telle bétise
Se peut-il qu'on nous dise.
Que sert d'en savoir tant?

MOT DE SOCRATE
Fable XX (Sur l'Air, "Du Cap de bonne esperance" — Air VII du Iᵉʳ Recueil)
(see p 51)
(Bon Amis Rares)
English summary on p. 168

I
Jadis un illustre Sage
C'est Socrate, nous dit-on,
Avoit fait pour son usage
Elever une maison.
Elle étoit peu magnifique
Sans colonne ni portique
Tout pour la comodité
Et rien pour la vanité.

II
Le grand nombre la méprise;
Le petit nombre applaudit;
Plusieurs trouvent qu'a leur
  guise
Le Logis est trop petit:
Las de tout ce verbiage,
Plût au Ciel, répond le Sage,
Tout petit qu'est ce logis,
Qu'il fut plein de vrais amis.

LE LION TERRASSÉ EN PEINTURE
Fable XXI (Sur l'Air, "Pour passer doucement la vie" — Air VII du Ier Recueil)

Fable XXI (Sur l'Air, "Pour passer doucement la vie" — Air VII du Ier Recueil)
(Les Fanfarons)
English summary on p. 168-169

I
On expossit une peinture,
Où l'Artisan voit tracé
Un Lion d'immense stature
Par un seul Homme terrassé.

II
Les Spectateurs en tiroient gloire,
Se récriant sur le haut fait.
Un Lion passa, dit l'histoire,
Et rabatit bien leur caquet.

III
L'art et la liberté de feindre,
Leur dit-il, vous ont tous deçus.
Si mes confreres savoient
   peindre,
L'Homme n'auroit pas le dessus.

LE SERPENT, ET LE VILLAGEOIS
Fable XXII (sur le même Air)
(L'Ingratitude)
English summary on p. 169

I
Il est bon d'être charitable:
Mais on risque à l'être sans
   choix.
Jadis un Serpent, dit la Fable,
En convainquit un Villageois.

II
Dans son sein cet Homme facile
Le reçut déja demi mort:
Et pour loyer l'ingrat Reptile
Contre lui s'elança d'abord.

III
Mal en prit à la laide bête:
C'est le fruit de tels attentats.
Le Manant lui trancha la tête
Belle leçon pour les ingrats.

VOLUME FIVE

LE VIEILLARD, ET SES ENFANS
Fable I (Sur l'Air, "L'autre jour j'apperçus etc")
(La Concorde)
English summary on p. 169

Vol. V/Ier Air
Légèrement

Ja - dis à Sparte, ou bien à Ro-me(N'im-porte en quel de ces deux lieux)

Al-loit mou-rir un Hom-me vieux: C'é-toit un sage et voi-ci comme, Se-lon l'his-

toi-re de-son tems, Il le fit voir à ses En-fans.

<table>
<tr><td align="center">II</td><td align="center">III</td></tr>
<tr><td>Près de son lit il les assemble:
Il avoit là trente batons,
Et de plusieurs tours de cordons
Les ayant fait lier ensemble,
Voyons, dit-il, qui de vous trois
Rompra ces verges à la fois.</td><td>Ils y perdirent tous leur peine
Alors sourit le bon Vieillard.
Rompez, dit-il, rompez la hard*
Qui les unit et les enchaine:
Les uns des autres divisés,
Ces jets seront bientôt brisés.</td></tr>
</table>

IV
Souvenez-vous de cet emblême,
Mes chers Enfans, soyez unis.
Tant qu'ils suivirent son avis,
Leur force fut la force-même:
Mais l'interêt les divisa,
Et qui voulut les écrasa.

*Corde

LE CHEVAL, LE CERF, ET L'HOMME
Fable II (sur le même Air)
(Remede pire que le mal)
English summary on p. 169

I

Quand on se livre à la vengeance,
On ne sçait gueres ce qu'on fait.
Mais dans la suite un vain regret
En fait sentir la conséquence.
Le Cheval fut ainsi dompté,
Et pleure encor sa liberté.

II

Avec un Cerf plein de vitesse
Il se brouilla pour la boisson:
Et n'en pouvant avoir raison,
Il eut recours à notre
   espece,*
Qui le brida, monta dessus,
Et depuis ne le lâcha plus.

*l'Homme

LES DEUX CHIENS, ET LEUR MAÎTRE
Fable III (Sur l'Air, "L'autre jour m'allant promener")
(L'Education)
English summary on p. 169

Vol. V/IIe Air

Légèrement

Un Per - son - na - ge   de re - nom,   Gen - til   homme et

B.C. en musette

ri - che, dit - on,   En - tre - te - noit   un   Chien mig - non,

Fai - ne-ant,   i - nu - ti - le,   Et   sa - chant pour

tou - te le - çon   L'ac - com-pag - ner en   vil - le.

II

Cet Homme avoit un autre
　　Chien,
Moins chéri, quoi que chassant
　　bien,
Et ne manquant jamais en rien
Ni d'ardeur ni d'adresse,
Tellement que par son moyen
Gibier venoit sans cesse.

III

Mais du gibier qu'on apprêtoit,
Chien chasseur jamais ne tatoit:
Et Chien oisif s'en ragoutoit
A la table du Maître,
Dans le tems qu'à l'autre on jet-
　　toit
Pain bis par la fenêtre.

IV

Fort mécontent de ce train là,
Qu'est-ce donc, dit-il, que cela?
Pour ce belître que voila
Sans chommer je travaille:
Et lui seul se dorlotant là,
Par mes soins fait ripaille.

V

Roger Bontems qui l'entendit,
Sans rancune lui répondit,
C'est notre Maître qui vous fit
A la fatigue austere,
Et qui, sage ou non, ne m'apprit
Qu'à manger sans rien faire.

VI

Quand on reproche aux jeunes
　　gens
D'être ignares et faineans,
Visiblement à leurs parens
La satire s'adresse.
Que veut-on que soient des en-
　　fans
Qu'on n'instruit ni ne dresse?

VII

La Fable encore nous apprend
Que les grands services qu'on
　　rend
Ne sont payés le plus souvent
Que d'un mince salaire,
Et qu'on gagne communément
Moins à servir qu'à plaire.

LA CHAUVE-SOURIS, ET LES DEUX BÉLETTES
Fable IV (sur le même Air)
(La Duplicité)
English summary on p. 169

I
Au lieu de son obscur taudis,
Une sotte Chauve-Souris
S'en alla prendre le logis
D'une fiere Bélette,
Qui traitoit les rats d'ennemis,
Et cherchoit leur défaite.

II
Qu'ai-je apperçu, dit celle-ci?
N'est-ce pas un Rat que ceci?
L'autre répond, criant merci,
Les Rats ont-ils des ailes?
Regardez de près, en voici:
J'en ai deux des plus belles.

III
Sans la trop bien considerer,
On la laisse se retirer:
Elle dabord de démarer,
Mais bientôt l'étourdie
Chez une autre alla se fourrer
Des Oiseaux ennemie.

IV
Qu'ai-je apperçu, dit celle-ci?
N'est-ce pas Oiseaux que ceci?
L'autre repond, criant merci,
Les Oiseaux ont plumage.
Je suis Rat, pour preuve voici
Le poil de mon corsage.

V
Ainsi deux fois elle échapa,
Et deux fois Bélettes dupa:
En riant elle décampa
L'impudente commere.
Je ne sçai quand on lui coupa
Sa langue mensongere.

VI
C'est en vain que vous triom-
      phez,
Grands menteurs et fourbes
      fieffés:
Et vainement vous vous coiffez
De votre sçavoir faire:
Chacun veut vous voir
      étouffez,
Et votre race entiere.

LE SOURICEAU, ET SA MERE
Fable V (Sur l'Air, "Le printems rappelle aux armes" — Vol. II, Air IV) (see p. 71)
(La mine trompe)
English summary on p. 169

I
Racontons l'étourderie
   Et l'ânerie,
Racontons l'étourderie
   D'un jeune Rat,
Qui disoit, Je meurs d'envie
D'aller embrasser le Chat.

II
Je le trouve tout aimable,
   Tout agréable
Je le trouve tout aimable,
   Tranquile et doux;
En on mot aux Rats semblable,
S'il n'étoit plus grand que nous.

III
Mais voyez quelle arrogance,
   Quelle insolence,
Mais voyez quelle arrogance
   Montre le Coq.
Je demeure en sa presence
Immobile comme un roc.

IV
Il eût poussé davantage
   Son verbiage,
Il eut poussé davantage
   Ses vains propos;
Mais sa Mere fine et sage
L'interrompit par ces mots.

V
Laisse-là ce Chatemite,
   Cet hipocrite:
Laisse-là ce Chatemite,
   Ce traitre Chat,
Qui n'a rien dans sa marmite
S'il n'y met Souris ou Rat.

VI
Mais du Coq souvent je dine
   Dans ma cuisine,
Mais du Coq souvent je dine
   Bien largement.
Il ne faut pas sur la mine
Pronouncer si promtement.

LE CERF, ET LA BREBIS
Fable VI (Sur l'Air, "Savetier qui toujours chante")
(Caution sujette à caution)
English summary on p. 169

Vol. V/IIIᵉ Air
Légèrement

B.C. en musette

Pre- tez -moi, je vous con - ju - re, Si nous som- mes bon a - mis, De vot- re grain u- ne dou- ble me- su- re Di- soit un jour le cerf à la Bre- bis.

	II		III
	Je me pique avec constance		La Brebis sentant le piége,
	D'être Cerf de bonne foi:		Répondit de fort bon sens:
	Mais s'il le faut pour plus grande		Tel emprunteur assorti d'un tel
	assurance,		pleige*
	Messire Loup va répondre pour		N'a pas trop l'air de payer dans
	moi.		le tems.

*Caution

L'ANE, ET SES MAÎTRES
Fable VII (sur le même Air)
(L'amour du changement)
English summary on p. 170

I	II
Quoi toujours avant l'aurore	Le Destin m'a-t-il fait naître
Se lever pour charier,	Pour n'avoir que du malheur?
Ou pour porter une franche	Le Destin donc lui donne un
pécore	autre Maître
Disoit un jour l'Ane d'un jar-	Notre Bourique est chez un Cor-
dinier.	royeur.

III

Aussitôt plainte nouvelle:
Que ces cuirs sentent mauvais!
Passe l'odeur: mais la voiture est
    telle,
Qu'à chaque pas il fléchit sous
    le faix.

IV

Bostangi* disoit la Bête,
Que ne suis-je encor chez vous!
Au moins, au moins quand vous
    tourniez la tête,
Je grignotois quelques fueilles
    de choux.

V

Mais ici jamais d'aubeine,
Ni relache, ni quartier.
Le Sort encor est sensible à sa
    peine,
Et pour Seigneur lui donne un
    Charbonnier.

VI

Le Baudet encor de braire,
Cris encor plus éclatans.
Nous voila tous: rien ne fait
    notre affaire.
Toujours changer: jamais n'être
    contens.

*Jardinier

L'AIGLE, ET LE RENARD
Fable VIII (Sur l'Air, "Où s'en vont ces gais Bergers?")
(Point de petit Ennemi)
English summary on p. 170

Vol. V/IVe Air

Légèrement

Au Re - nard l'Aigle a -voit pris L'es - poir de sa fa - mil -

B.C. en musette

le, Je veux di - re ses pe - tits, Et se moc - quoit du dril -

le, Qui di - soit en pou-ssant les hauts cris, A l'ai - de! On me pil - le.

II

Puis sur ce ton de douceur
Qu'on prend lorsqu'on supplie,
S'adressant au ravisseur,
Humblement il le prie.
Lui disant, Rendez-moi,
    Monseigneur,
Mes enfans et al vie.

III

Sur le haut d'un Pin perché,
L'Auteur de sa misere
De ses pleurs n'est point
    touché,
Il rit de sa priere,
Au milieu de ses Aiglons niché,
Chantant, Lere lanlere.

IV

Le Renard ne gagnant rien
Alors dit en lui-même
N'ai-je pas quelque moyen
Dans ma finesse extrême?
Oh! si fait. Il le trouva fort bien:
Voici le stratagême.

V

Dans un temple tout voisin
Brule une torche ardente
Il l'empoigne et court au Pin
Dont l'Hôte s'épouvante,
Trop heureux de rendre le butin
Et que l'on s'en contente.

VI

Ca, dit-il, faisons la paix:
Arrête l'incendie:
De bon coeur je te remets
Ta famille chérie.
Le Renard dit, Tope, et chante
    après
Avec l'Aigle en partie.

VII

Quelque grand que vous soyez
Craignez de faire offense
Aux petits que vous voyez
Sans force et sans deffense.
Vous errez, si vous ne les croyez
Capables de vengence.

Facsimile of Fable ix, Volume V (opposite).

LA TORTUE, ET L'AIGLE
Fable IX (Sur l'Air, "Quelque vent qui gronde")
(Vanité Opiniatre)
English summary on p. 170

Vol. V/Ve Air
Légèrement

L'a - ni-mal, dit - on, Qui por-te sa mai - son sur son chig-non, Et dont le corps n'est ni chalr ni pois - son, Bref Da - me Tor - tu - e, De cha-cun con - nu - e Par sa fa - çon d'al - ler, Vou-lut ap-prendre à vo - ler, Bref da-me Tor - tu - e, De cha-cun con-nu - e Par sa fa-çon d'a - ller, Vou-lut ap-prendre à vo - ler.

II

L'innocente donc
Alla prendre leçon
D'un maître Aiglon,
Dans ce métier Oiseau de grand
    renom:
Lui d'abord d'en rire,
Et puis de lui dire:
Cessez de vous tromper:
Vous ne pouvez que ramper.

III

C'est votre destin:
Quittez votre dessein:
Il est trop vain,
Et trop nouveau, trop dangereux
    enfin.
Mais Dame Tortue,
De chacun connue
Par sa façon d'aller,
Voulut apprendre à voler.

IV

Las de ses propos,
L'Oiseau lui dit ces mots,
(Avis aux sots)
A vos périls mettez-vous sur
    mon dos.
Dans l'air il la guinde
Plus haut que le Pinde,*
Et puis la plante là:
Jugez comme elle vola.

V

J'ai vû maint faquin,
Encor blanc du moulin,
Allant grand train,
Bien haut grimpé dégringoler
    soudain:
Comme la Tortue,
Follement têtue,
Qui pour dégrigoler
Voulut apprendre à voler.

*Montagne fort haute

LE LION, ET LA GRENOUILLE
Fable X (sur le même Air)
(Le Clabaudeur)
English summary on p. 170

I

Le Roi des forets
Ouït dans un marais,
Passant auprès,
Certain voix que nous dirons
    après
Voix sonnante et pleine,
Et qui dans la plaine
Faisoit un si grand bruit,
Qu'on n'en dormoit point la nuit.

IV

Approchons pourtant,
Dit-il, en rugissant,
Et s'avançant
Dans les roseaux et le limon glis-
    sant.
Mais tandis qu'il fouille,
Il voit la Grenouille,
Qui fait toujours le cri
Dont il étoit ébahi.

II

Qu'est-ce que cela?
Dit le Lion, hola!
Qu'entens-je là?
Est-ce un Tiphon?** c'est-ce un
Gargantua**
Quoi que ce puisse être,
Je veux le connoître:
Soit hydre, soit dragon,
Fera-t'on peur au Lion?

** Géans

V

D'abord il en rit,
Et puis il en rougit,
Non sans dépit
De s'être ainsi laissé surpren-
    dre au bruit
Enfin il écrase
La bête à l'emphase
Qui crie autant qu'un boeuf,
Etant moins grosse qu'un oeuf.

III

Quoi que plein de coeur,
De force, et de valeur,
Ce grand veneur
Ne laisse pas d'avoir quelque
    frayeur.
Ce qui plus l'étonne,
C'est que ni personne,
Ni bête dans ces lieux
Ne se découvre à ses yeux.

VI

Parmi les humains
On en trouve certains
Tout aussi vains:
De loin Géans, de près cirons
    ou nains.
Un criard résonne:
On croit qu'il raisonne.
On dit: C'est un Docteur:
Et ce n'est qu'un Clabaudeur.

LES OISONS, ET LES PIGEONS
Fable XI (sur le même Air)
(Aux riches les voleurs)
English summary on p. 170

I

Avec gras Oisons
Paissoient dans les sillons
Maigres Pigeons,
Quand il survint cohorte de lar-
  rons:
Les enfans de l'Oye
Furent seuls en proye:
Leurs compagnons légers
Prirent l'esor dans les airs.

II

Quand les ennemis
Ravagent un pays
Qu'ils ont soumis,
Qui risque plus? les grands, ou
  les petits?
Dans cette avanture
J'en vois la figure;
Les grands sont les Oisons,
Et les petits les Pigeons.

LA MOUCHE, ET LA FOURMI
Fable XII (Sur l'Air, "Tous les Bourgeois de Châtres")
(Sotte Vanité)
English summary on p. 170

Je suis, di- soit la Mou - che, A la ta- ble des Rois: Dans

leur pa - lais je cou - che, Et mê - me quel - que fois. Je

per - che sur leur nez, J'y dan - se, je m'y jou - e. D'un pe - tit air mig-

non, Don don, Tan - tôt cy tan - tôt là, La La, Je les pince à la jou - e

II

Pour toi, chétif insecte,
Dit-elle à la Fourmi,
Dans ta demeure abjecte
Tu ne vis qu'à demi:
A peine les Bourgeois te don-
    nent quelque entrée
Dans le coin d'un sillon, Don
    don,
Loin de ces Messieurs-là La la,
L'on te voit enterrée.

III

Oui, dit la Ménagere:
Mais j'y suis en repos,
Sans froid et sans misere,
Sans aucun de tes maux:
Et quand à tes beaux jeux (bien
    sot qui les envie)
Même avec la Guenon Don don,

Jouant comme cela, La la,
N'y perds-tu pas la vie?

IV

Plusieurs par le frivole
Se vantent d'être heureux:
Et dans leur tête folle,
Tout est au dessous d'eux.
Laissons-les à leur gré se
    bercer dans le vuide:
Ni le beau ni le bon Don don,
Jamais ne se trouva La la,
Sinon dans le solide.

LA LAITIERE
Fable XIII (sur le même Air)
(Les Châteaux en Espagne)
English summary on p. 170

I

A son chemin Pérette
Portant un pot au lait,
Croit vendre, faire emplette
Et fortune à souhait.
Mais sautant de plaisir, le pied
    dont elle danse,
Tient mal sur le talon Don don,
Et le lait tombant là La la,
Fait tomber l'espérance.

II

De Châteaux en Espagne
Est rempli l'univers:
Chacun bat la campagne
Et bâtit dans les airs.
Mais tandis que l'esprit cherche
    à se satisfaire
Toujours quelque Démon Don
    don,
Qui se trouve par là La la,
Améne le contraire.

LE BLÉ, LES MOUTONS, LES LOUPS, ET LES HOMMES
Fable XIV (Sur l'Air, "Jeunesse qui dans vos beaux ans")
(Rien de trop)
English summary on p. 171

Vol. V/VIIe **Air**

Le Blé trop é-pais et touf-fu En in-u-ti-li-tes s'é-puis-se. Pour en ô-ter le su-per-flu, La Gent bê-lan-te fut com-mi-se: Mais ne de-vant qu'un peu brou-ter, Mou-tons al-le-rent tout gâ-ter.

B.C. en musette

II	**III**
Pour les punir fut dit aux Loups:	Alors à l'Homme il fut permis
Exercez sur eux la vengeance:	De faire à ces gloutons-la guerre
Mais n'allez pas les manger tous.	Armé contre ces ennemis
Suivirent-ils bien l'ordonnance?	Il veut en dépeupler la terre:
Ils en croquèrent à tel point,	Car d'être juste et modéré,
Qu'ils n'en laisserent presque point.	Chez les humains est ignoré.

IV

Petits et grands sont dans le cas.
Fuyez l'excès, c'est la maxime:
Mais on ne la pratique pas,
Quoi qu'on la vante et qu'on l'estime
Toujours on préche cette loi;
On ne la prend jamais pour soi.

LE SERPENT, ET LA LIME
Fable XV (sur le même Air)
(L'Envie)
English summary on p. 171

I

On dit que chez un Horloger,
Par une assez rare avanture,
Un serpent cherchant à manger;
N'y trouva qu'une Lime dure:
Comme il pensoit la grignoter,
La Lime se mit à chanter.

II

Tu t'en prens à plus dur que toi,
Petit Serpent à tète folle.
Plutôt que d'emporter de moi
Seulement le quart d'une obole,
Tu te romprois toutes les dents:
Je ne crains que celles du tems.

III

De la Vertu tel est le sort:
Elle redoute peu l'Envie
Et loin d'en craindre quelque tort,
Elle se rit de sa furie.
Tous les traits qu'on peut lui lancer,
Jamais ne peuvent la blesser.

LES LOUPS, ET LES BREBIS
Fable XVI (Sur l'Air, "Tout ce qui respire")
(Paix fourrée)
English summary on p. 171

II

Pour notre assurance,
Poursuivent les Loups,
Vos chiens parmi nous
Feront résidence,
Bien entretenus
Sur nos revenus.

III

Louvants* des plus sages
De notre coté
Seront du traité,
Chez vous de surs gages,
Au Berger soumis
Sur le pied d'amis.

*Jeunes loups

IV

On fait donc l'échange:
Matins désormais
Ont gîte aux forets,
Louvats à la grange,
Tous des plus petits;
Mais bons apprentis.

V

Mauvaise herbe à croître
Met fort peu de tems:
Louvats bientôt grands
Font leurs coups de maître,
Si bien que Loups vieux
N'auroient pas fait mieux.

VI

De la bergerie
Le Gardien absent,
De peuple bélant
Ils font boucherie.
Ah! quel abbatis
D'Agneaux et Brebis!

VII

Les drôles s'enfuirent
Chargés de butin:
Un bois est voisin:
C'est là qu'ils se mirent,
S'y tenant cachés,
Et bien retranchés.

VIII

L'un d'eux à leurs Maîtres
Va dire le fait:
On le tient secret
A la cour des traîtres,
Jusqu'au lendemain,
Qu'on vit leur dessein.

IX

Des chiens en ôtage
Qui dormoient la nuit
Sans faire de bruit
Ils firent carnage.
Tel fut le succès
Du traité de paix.

X

La paix doit nous plaire:
Elle est bonne en soi.
Avec gens sans foi
Faut-il donc la faire?
Non, c'est le panneau
Qui perd le troupeau.

LES PIGEONS, ET LE MILAN
Fable XVII (sur le même Air)
(Paix fourrée)
English summary on p. 171

I

Bien sot qui se fie
A son ennemi;
Mais sot et demi
Qui s'y sacrifie,
Comme les Pigeons
Qu'ici nous chantons.

II

Leur aîle légere
Trompant le Milan,
L'avide tiran
N'en attrapoit guere,
C'etoit deux ou trois
En cinq ou six mois.

III

Enfin à la ruse
Le traître a recours:
Et par beaux discours
Méchament abuse
Les bons idiots:
Et leur dit ces mots:

IV

Messieurs, plus de guerre
Ni noise entre nous.
Je suis tout à vous
De bec et de serre,
Pour vous protéger,
Et pour vous venger.

V

Sous ma coulevrine
Vous vivrez en paix:
Bravant désormais
Oiseaux de rapine.
Epreviers, Autours,
Et même Vautours.

VI

Par tant d'amour, Sire,
Et tant de bonté,
Votre Majesté
Mérite l'empire,
A l'instant répond
Le peuple Pigeon.

VII

Le voila donc maître,
Et maître absolu,
Et maître goulu,
Autant qu'il veut l'être
Jugez quel dégat
Fait le scélérat.

VIII

Tout sent les atteintes
De son appétit.
Et tout retentit
D'inutiles plaintes.
Là conduit l'erreur:
Avis au lecteur.

LE FOU QUI VEND LA SAGESSE

Fable XVIII (Sur l'Air, "Nos plaisir seront peu durables"—Air IX, Ier Recueil (see p. 53)
(Avec les Fous point de commerce)
English summary on p. 171

I

Certain Fou vendoit la Sagesse,
Ou du moins disoit: Je la vends.
D'acheter le monde s'empresse,
Et court sur tout aux Charlatans.

II

Celui-ci fait mille grimaces,
Puis vous baille en vous soufletant
Un fil long de deux ou trois brasses
Pour bel et bon argent comptant.

III

Si quelqu'un se met en colere,
Il s'en moque et lui rit au nez:
Vous avez, dit-il, votre affaire:
Allez-vous-en, et devinez.

IV

Que comprendre à tout ce grimoire?
Dans le fond a-t'il quelque sens?
Un fort bon: vous le pouvez croire,
Au sentiment d'habiles gens.

V

Ils diront, si l'on les consulte,
Soyez loin de l'impertinent:
Qui le suit, s'expose à l'insulte,
Y perd l'honneur avec l'argent.

VI

La longueur du fil qu'on vous laisse,
Marque bien cet éloignement.
En ce point paroît la Sagesse;
Ce Fou la vend assurément.

L'AIGLE, ET LE HIBOU
Fable XIX (Sur l'Air, "Vous qui vous moquez par vos ris" — Air XI, IIᵉ Recueil)
(see p. 81)
(Amour aveugle)
English summary on p. 171-72

I
Au dernier point tout Pere est fou
De sa progeniture,
Quand elle auroit d'un Loup-garou
La façon et l'allure.
Ecouter comme le Hibou
Des siens fait la peinture.

II
Que tous les genres des Oiseaux
Aux miens portent envie:
Ils sont mignons, bien faits, et
  beaux,
D'une grace accomplie,
En tout parfaits originaux
Qui n'ont point de copie.

III
A l'Aigle il fait ce beau portrait
De sa hideuse engeance,
Afin que s'il la recontroit
Il usât d'indulgence:
Car las de guerre ils avoient fait
Un traité d'alliance

IV
Mais l'Aigle un soir étant aux
  champs,
Trouve en une mazure
De petits monstres grimaçans,
Et d'horrible figure,
Les yeux hagards et menaçons,
La laideur toute pure.

V
Je sçai fort bien de notre ami
Qu'elle est, dit-il, la race:
Ceux-ci n'en ont air ni demi:
Devons-nous faire grace?
Nenni vraiment, vraiment nenni,
Mais au plutôt main basse.

VI
A son retour Messer Hibou
Ne trouvant que carnage,
Se désespere dans son trou
De douleur et de rage:
L'air retentit de ses hou hou
Dans tout le voisinage.

VII
Pour comble aucun ne te plaignit
Sachant son avanture:
Mais ce qu'à l'Aigle il avoit dit,
Fut mis dans le Mercure:
Et le Pont-neuf en retentit
De Robin lure lure.

VOLUME SIX

LES GRENOUILLES QUI DEMANDENT UN ROI
(L'Amour du changement)
Fable I (Sur l'Air de l'Esprit)
English summary on p. 172

II

Le premier qu'on leur donna
Fut un manche de charue.
Il fit peur quand il tomba,
Et chacune en fut émue;
Mais bientôt, (bis) le voyant coi,
Il faut voir comme on le hue,
Mais bientôt, (bis) le voyant coi,
On demande un autre Roi.

III

A la place du perdus
En vient un qui se remue,
Et qui vole, c'est bien plus:
En un mot, c'est une Grue;
Et d'abord, (bis) Sa Majesté
Fait main basse, croque, tue,
Et d'abord, (bis) Sa Majesté
Fait haïr sa Royauté.

IV

Et Grenouilles de prier
Qu'on leur donne un autre Sire:
Mais ou les laissa crier;
Se contentant de leur dire
Dépendez, (bis) de celui-là,
De peur qu'il n'en vienne un pire,
Dépendez, (bis) de celui-là;
Et l'affaire finit là.

LE RHETEUR, ET LE ROI
Fable II (Sur l'Air, "Mon Pere étoit, etc.")
(Les Charlatans)
English summary on p. 172

Vol. VI/IIe Air
Légèrement

Ça di-soit un Rhé-teur, Que l'on m'a-méne un A-ne, Et j'en fais un Doc-teur, Doc-teur por-tant sou-la-ne, Ex-pert, Sa-vant, et di-sert.

B.C. en musette

II
Le prince avoit chez lui
Un Roussin d'Arcadie,
Et dit: Dès aujourdhui
Je veux qu'il étudie.
  Venez,
Et l'entreprenez.

III
Combien faut-il de tems
Pour mettre à fin l'ouvrage?
Il ne faut que dix ans,
Répond le Personage,
  Plus fin
Que le Souverain.

IV
Mais pour bien commencer,
Poursuit notre habile homme,
Vous devez financer
Considérable somme.
  Le Roi
Avoit bien dequoi.

V
Il fait donner l'argent
Mais avec clause expresse,
Qu'on pende le Regent,
S'il manque à sa promesse.
  Soit fait,
Dit maître Caquet.

VI
Chacun le crut perdu:
Mais il ne fit qu'en rire.
Pour n'être point pendu,
Sçut-il alors bien dire,
  Dix ans
Sont mes surs garans.

VII
Pour éluder la loi
Le terme est salutaire,
L'Ane, le Sire, ou moi
Mourrons avant l'affaire.
  Ce mot
N'étoit pas d'un sot.

VIII

Ainsi le Courtisan,
Et quelquefois le Prince
Sont par le Charlatan,
Comme gens de province,
  Menez
Et priz par le nez.

LE CHEVAL, ET L'ANE
Fable III (sur le même Air)
(L'Inhumanité)
English summary on p. 172

I

Un cheval peu courtois
S'égayoit en voyage.
N'ayant que son harnois,
Tandis que du baggage
  Baudet
Portoit le paquet.

II

L'Ane accablé, confus,
Et baissant les oreilles,
Lui dit: Je n'en puis plus;
Et de ces deux corbeilles
  Le poids
Me met aux abois.

III

Ce ne sera que jeu
Pour votre Seigneurie:
Prenez au moins un peu
Du fardeau, je vous prie.
  Sans quoi,
C'en est fait de moi.

IV

Le Roussin répondit
Par mainte pétarade
Tant qu'à la fin il rit
Son pauvre camarade
  Mourir,
Sans le secourir.

V

Il auroit bien mieux fait
D'écouter la priere:
On lui mit du Baudet
La charge toute entiere
  Dessus,
Et la peau de plus.

VI

Qu'il est de ces chevaux
Sous la figure humaine,
Qui riant de nos maux,
Loin de s'en mettre en peine,
  Nous font
Affront sur affront.

VII

C'est tous les jours ainsi
Que les petits succombent:
Mais il arrive aussi
Que leurs fardeaux retõbent
  Sur ceux,
Qui se moquoient d'eux.

LE LOUP, LA MERE ET L'ENFANT
Fable IV (Sur l'Air de la Régence, ou "Tout le long de la rivière")
(Folle attente)
English summary on p. 172

Vol. VI/III Air

U - ne bon - ne Me- re, Son Mar - mot pleu - rant, Pour le fai - re

B.C. en musette

tra - ite, Lui dit en gron - dant Je m'en vais, je te le ju - re, Te don-

ner au Loup: Et le Loup par a - van - tu - re, Pa-rut tout - à - coup.

II

La gloutonne Bête
Attend le Poupon:
Et d'en faire fête
Compte tout de bon.
L'Idiot peut-être pense
Qu'après le serment,
On lui doit en conscience
Ce contentement.

III

Mais le pauvre Here
En sçavoit bien peu;
Juremens de Mere
Sont traitez de jeu:
Ce n'est que pure grimace
Qu'alors elle fait:
La colere et la menace
Furent sans effet.

IV

Le Loup sur la porte
Etant apperçu,
De la bonne sorte
Est bientôt reçu:
Le mâtin sort et l'acroche
De ses grosses dents:
Et les gens à coups de broche
Lui percent les flans.

LE LOUP ET LA CICOGNE
Fable V (sur le même Air)
(L'Ingratitude des Grands)
English summary on p. 172-73

I
Mangeant à sa guise,
Un Loup grand glouton,
Eut la gorge prise
D'un os de mouton:
Par bonheur une Cicogne
Vint tout à propos;
Et s'étant mise en besogne,
Lui tira cet os.

II
Pour un tel service,
Le plus grand de tous,
Dit l'Opératrice,
Que me donnez-vous?
Ton salaire c'est la vie,
Répondit le Loup;
Je ne te l'ai point ravie:
N'est-ce pas beaucoup?

III
Ton col sans domage
De ma gueule sort;
Vouloir d'avantage
N'as-tu pas grand tort?
Quelqu'office qu'on nous rende,
A nous autres Grands,
La récompense est trop grande
D'éviter nos dents.

LE TORRENT, ET LA RIVIÈRE

Fable VI (Sur l'Air, "Flamans, à votre secours")
(Les Sournois)
English summary on p. 173

A grand bruit, à grand fra- cas tom-boit de haut en bas

Un fier tor - rent qu'u - ne mon - ta - gne De ses en - trail - les vo - mis -

soit. La cam - pag - ne Re-ten-tis-soit, Et de loin L'an- non- çoit.

II

Poursuivi par un brigand,
Fuyoit certain marchand:
Il rencontra cette barriere
Et la franchit avec bonheur:
L'onde fiere
Sans profondeur
Ne lui fit point de peur.

III

Le voleur aussi passé,
L'Homme est encor pressé:
Une Rivière se présente;
Qui sans murmure allant son train,
Douce et lente
Semble un bassin
Uni comme la main.

IV

L'Homme crut, et crut fort mal,
Sans danger ce canal:
Il y trouve un profound abime:
A le passer il se roidit,
Il s'anime
Sans aucun fruit:
Le gouffre l'engloutit.

V

Des Sournois défions-nous:
Ils font sans bruit leurs coups.
Une humeur vive impétueuse
Nous avertit par ses éclats:
La rêveuse
Trame tout bas
Ses cruels attentats.

LE LEVRAUT, ET LA TORTUE
Fable VII (sur le même Air)
(Hâtez-vous lentement)
English summary on p. 173

I
Qui ne part au point certain,
Court et galope en vain.
Que l'on s'anime et s'évertue,
Rien ne corrige ce défaut:
   La Tortue
   Se rend plutôt
Au but que le Levraut.

II
Il savoient gagé tous deux
Et mis de bons enjeux.
Allez toujours, dit le Compere,
Il ne me faut que deux instans:
   La Comere
   Prend les devans
Et ne perd point de tems.

III
Le Coureur la voit enfin
Presqu'au bout du chemin:
Comme un trait part de l'arbalête,
Il part, il vole, mais sans fruit:
   Et la bête
   Dit on perdit
L'honneur et le profit.

LE TRÉSOR, ET LES DEUX HOMMES
Fable VIII (sur l'Air, "Encor un tour de broche")
(L'Avarice)
English summary on p. 173

C'est u - ne tra - ge - di - e, Que je vais vous chan -

ter, Peut - ê - tre co - mé - di - e, Per - mis à vous d'op - ter.

Quand il s'a - git d'a - va - res, Les plus é - tran - ges

cas, Tou - jours sont si bi - zar - res, Que l'on nèn pleu - re pas.

II
De sa misere extrême
Un Gueux cherchant la fin,
De s'étrangler lui même
Conçut le beau dessein:
Au haut d'une mazure
Il va planter un clou,
Et de juste mesure
Y dispose un licou.

III
Mais tandis qu'il travaille
Pour se donner la mort,
S'éboule la muraille
Enceinte d'un trésor:
Il le prend sans attendre,
Laissant là le cordeau,
Dont il alloit se pendre
Sans ce secours nouveau.

IV

Le mur dépositaire
N'a tombe pas sans bruit,
Et le propriétaire
Ne dort gueres la nuit.
Il vient à grande course
Mais il vient un peu tard,
Et cherchant une bourse,
Ne trouve qu'une hard.*

V

Encore patience,
Dit-il, j'épargne un sou:
On à fait la dépense
Pour moi de ce licou.
Il dit, et sans attendre
S'attache le cordeau,
Et s'aide pour se pendre
De ce secours nouveau.

*Corde

LE COQ, ET LA PERLE
Fable IX (sur le même Air)
(Marché donné)
English summary on p. 173

I

J'ai fait une trouvaille,
Disoit jadis un Coq.
Qui veut, vaille que vaille,
Avec moi faire un troc?
C'est une Perle fine:
Mais j'aime mieux, dit-il,
Avoir pour ma cuisine
Le moindre grain de mil.

II

Ouvrages d'importance,
Peintures, manuscrits,
Aux yeux de l'ignorance
Sont toujours de vil prix.
Qu'une antique médaille
Soit chez un Villageois;
Le sot, quoi qu'elle vaille,
Ne la vendra qu'au poids.

L'HIRONDELLE, ET LE ROSSIGNOL

Fable X (Sur l'Air, "J'entens déja le bruit des arnes.") (see p. 147)
(Point de belle prison)

English summary on p. 173

Vol. VI/VI Air
Légèrement

Au-tre-fois pour voir *Phi-lo-me-le, **Pro-gné dans les bois

B.C. en musette

s'en al-la: Elle y trou-va sa soeur fi-de-le

Qui chan-toit re mi fa sol la; Que fai-tes - vous, ma

soeur, dit-el-le, Dans ce de-sert où vous voi-la?

*le Rossignol

**l'Hirondelle

	II	III	IV
	Ne savez-vous tant de musique,	Chez les Rois, chérie, admirée,	Ajoutez, répond la chanteuse,
	Que pour charmer des animaux,	Venez: vos jours seront heureux	Belle et triste captivité.
	Ou tout au plus quelque rustique,	Là vous aurez maison dorée,	Espererois-je d'être heureuse
	Qui n'entend point des chants si beaux,	Meuble et repas selon vos voeux,	Où je serois sans liberté?
	Et pour merci souvent s'applique	Et sans manquer chaque soirée	Toute prison est ennuyeuse:
	A vous happer dans ses réseaux?	L'amusement de mille jeux.	Tout esclavage détesté.

LE LOUP, ET LE CHIEN
Fable XI (Sur l'Air, "Ce n'est point par effort")
(La Liberté)
English summary on p. 173

II
Non, disoit le Loup de la Fable,
Au Chien bien gras, mais enchainé.
Pour moi ton sort n'est point
    aimable:
En vain tu te crois fortuné:
Si je suis maigre et misérable,
Du moins ne suis-je pas gené.

L'ECREVISSE, ET LA CHENILLE
Fable XII (sur le même Air)
(L'Exemple)
English summary on p. 173-74

I
L'Ecrevisse grondoit sa fille
De ce qu'elle n'alloit pas droit.
Certes, lui dit une Chenille,
Vous la tancez sans aucun droit:
Un enfant dans une famille
Ne peut faire que ce qu'il voit.

II
C'est l'exemple qui nous dirige:
Sans lui l'on sermone à l'envers.
C'est vainement que l'on corrige,
Quand on est soi même pervers.
Ira-t'on droit, quoi que l'exige
Celui qui marche de travers?

LA GRENOUILLE, ET LE RAT
Fable XIII (Sur l'Air, "Attendez-moi sous l'ornie"—Air VI, Ier Recueil), (see p. 50)
(La Perfidie)
English summary on p. 174

I
Sur une verte rive
Un Rat prenoit le frais.
Au même endroit arrive
L'Hostesse* des marais.
Que je me félicite
De vous trouver ici,
Lui dit cette hipocrite
D'un air tout radouci.

II
Venez, ajoute-l'elle
Vous rafraichir chez nous:
Ami, ma loge est belle,
Et les bains sont fort doux.
L'ami dit que sans aide
Il ne sauroit nager.
J'ai dit l'autre, un remede
Facile à ménager.

III
Un jonc fera l'affaire.
Vous vous attacherez
A mon pied de derriere
Et puis vous me suivrez
Fort bien: mais la perfide
Vouloit au fond de l'eau
De celui qu'elle guide
Faire un friand morceau.

IV
Il l'apperçoit, et crie
Ah! ne me noyez pas.
Mais c'est en vain qu'il prie:
Toujours on tire en bas.
Tandis qu'il se souléve
Encor tant mal que bien
Un Mitan vient, enléve
Rat, Grenouille, et lien.

V
Souvent la perfidie
Nuit à son propre Auteur:
Souvent la mieux ourdie
Fait son plus grand malheur:
Combien à la Grenouille
Semblables aujourd'hui
Se mettent en bredouille
En y mettant autrui.

*la Grenouille

L'ALOUETTE, L'AUTOR, ET L'OISELEUR

Fable XIV (Sur l'Air, "Tu dis qu'en, etc," or "Elle est de trop dãs le mõde")
(Point de quartier à qui n'en donne)
English summary on p. 174

II
C'est en vain qu'elle le prie:
Il la plume tout de bon.
Mais voici pendant qu'elle crie,
L'Oiseleur qui grippe le glouton.

III
Alors comme l'Alouette
Il a beau crier merci:
Comme il a traité l'on le traite.
Inhumains, n'oubliez pas ceci.

IV
Vous ne faites point de grace,
Doit-on vous en accorder?
Est-il juste qu'on vous en fasse?
Au Chasseur allez le demander.

LE CHAPON, ET LE FAUCON
Fable XV (sur le même Air)
(La Défiance)
English summary on p. 174

I
Un Chapon qu'on vouloit prendre
Pour en orner un festin,
N'étant pas d'avis de s'y rendre.
Vers les champs prit un essor sou-
dain.

II
Tous les gens de la cuisine
Disent Vien, petit, petit.
Il s'en moque, toujours chemine
Et loin d'eux de plus en plus s'en-
fuit.

III
Un Faucon veut l'entreprendre,
Et lui dit: Pouvre ignorant!
On ne peut jamais rien t'apprendre,
Mais pour moi je suis bien différent.

IV
Sur le poing de notre Maître
Quand il veut je sçais voler:
Il t'appelle de la fenêtre
Et vers lui tu ne veux pas aller.

V
Ah! tu me la bailles belle,
Lui répond le fin Mangeaur.
Irois-tu, si lors qu'on t'appelle,
L'on étoit armé d'un grand couteau.

LES BÂTONS FLOTTANS
Fable XVI (sur l'Air, "Tout cela m'est indifférent")
(L'Apparence)
English summary on p. 174

Vol. VI/IXᵉ Air
Légèrement

Quel qu'un vo - yant   de loin sur   l'eau   Flot - ter des   ver - ges

B.C. en musette

en   fais - ceau,   Cri - a   d'a - bord: C'est grand na - vi - re,

Et   puis ga - lere,   et puis bru - lot: Mais à   la   fin

il   fit bien   ri - re,   Quand il dit,   Ce n'est   qu'un   fa - got.

II
Il est au monde bien des gens
Qui de loin vous parvissent grands:
Qu'on les approche, c'est guenille,
Néant vêtu, frivole objet,
Ver qui reluit fêtu qui brille,
De tout mépris digne sujet.

LE DAUPHIN, ET LA GUENON
Fable XVII (sur le même Air)
(Le Sot menteur)
English summary on p. 174

I

Ce trait regarde le menteur,
Et je le tiens d'un bon Auteur,
Qui nous apprend qu'en un
naufrage
Auroient péri les Matelots,
Si maint Dauphin vers le rivage
Ne les eût porté sur son dos.

II

Comme l'un d'eux une Guenon
Vient se mettre à califourchon:
D'abord il la prend pour un
homme.
Mais en doutant peutêtre un peu,
Et l'interroge, et voici comme
Il lui fit décéler son jeu.

III

Estes-vous d'Athene ou d'Argos?
Elle repond à ces propos:
Je suis d'Athens la savante.
Ce n'étoit mentir qu'à demi;
Pour achiver elle se vanie
Que le Pyrée* est son ami.

IV

Quoi! pour un homme prendre un
port?
Dit le Dauphin, vous errez fort.
Mais que faisois-je aussi moi
même?
Croyant porter un Amphion**
Que ma bévue étoit extrême!
Je ne portois qu'une Guenon.

V

Je ne veux point d'un tel fardeau:
Laide menteuse, allez dans l'eau.
En même tems il l'y replonge:
Dame Guenache tombe au fond.
Aussi souvent le sot mensonge
Réussit à ceux qui le font.

*Port d'Athene
**Fameux Musician

LE SINGE ET LE CHAT
Fable XVIII (Sur l'Air, "Vous me l'avez dit, etc.")
(Les Fripons)
English summary on p. 174

Vol. VI/X Air
Gaiment

Ber- trand Sin - ge grand fri - pon, Et le Chat nom - mé Ra - ton.

B.C. en musette

Sce - le - rats fins et fa - meux, Dans u - ne mai - son Ha-bi-toient tous

deux Sce - le - rats fins et fa - meux, Et tou-jours d'ac- cord entre - eux.

II
Le premier de ces Larrons
Voyoit au feu des marrons.
Comment les avoir? par ou?
Nous vous les aurons,
Dit l'autre Filou,
Comment les avoir? par ou?
Le voici, dit le Matou.

III
Il écarte avec les doigts
Cendre et charbons à la fois.
Et chataignes de voler,
Là deux, ici trois,
On les voit rouler:
Et chataignes de voler,
Et le Singe d'embaler.

IV
Mais sans se bruler un peu,
Peut-on manier du feu?
Maître Chat de tems en tems
Souffroit de ce jeu.
Et grinçoit les dents:
Maître Chat de tems en tems
Poussoit quelques cris perçans.

V
A ce bruit le Marmiton
Accourt avec un bâton.
Le vol fut pour le Magot
Qui laissant Raton
S'enfuit au plustôt:
Le vol fut pour le Magot,
Et Raton paya l'écot.

LE BERGER, ET LE TROUPEAU
Fable XIX (sur le même Air)
(Faux Braves)
English summary on p. 175

I
Je perds, disoit Coridon,
Chaque jour quelque Mouton.
Eh quoi! je suis sans secours
Contre le Glouton
Qui me fait ces tours,
Eh quoi! je suis sans secours:
Et le serai-je toujours?

II
Mes Beliers dans leurs combats
Entre eux ne s'épargnent pas.
Et contre le Loup voleur
S'il faut faire un pas,
Ils tremblent de peur:
Et contre le Loup voleur
Ils n'ont ni force ni coeur.

III
A ces mots tout le Troupeau,
Jusqu'au plus petits Agneau,
S'écria: Comptez sur nous:
Contre le Boureau
Vous nous aurez tous:
S'écria: Comptez sur nous,
Quand il viendroit mille Loups.

IV
A quelques momens de là
Quelqu'un crie: Ah! le voila.
C'étoit ombre toutefois,
Et cette ombre là
Mit tout aux abois:
C'étoit ombre toutefois,
Qui sembloit venir des bois.

V
Eussiez-vous cent escadrons
D'Hommes laches et poltrons,
Au seul nom des ennemis
Tous vos fanfarons
Ont en vain promis,
Au seul nom des ennemis
Vos Geans sont des fourmis.

LE LOUP, ET LE CHEVAL
Fable XX (Sur l'Air, "Vous qui vous moquez par vos ris" — Air XI, (IIᵉ Recueil) (See p 81)
(Fourbe dupe)
English summary on p. 175

I
Un Loup vit un Cheval paissant
Au coin d'une prairie,
Un peu malade, mais puissant
Malgré sa maladie,
Et point du tout l'air innocent,
Ni la mine étourdie.

II
De haute lute le forcer
Etoit sans apparence
Le Loup voulant donc lui dresser
Un piége d'importance:
Pour Medecin vint s'announcer,
Et vanter sa science.

III
En charlatan il raconta
Mainte apocriphe histoire,
De cent Coursiers, qu'il inventa,
Gueris par son grimoire:
Et dans ce cas il se flata
D'en grossir le memoire.

IV
Regarde donc, dit le Cheval
Qui ne s'y fioit guere:
Un enclouture est tout mon mal:
C'est au pied de derriere.
Qui fut le sot? Le Marechal,
D'approcher la visiere.

V

Car le Poulain prenant son tems
Pour lacher la ruade,
Lui dit, c'est là que je t'attends,
Papelard camarade:
Et da sa gueule et de ses dents
Fit une marmelade.

VI

Tout fourbe doit manquer son
    coup,
Dès lors qu'on le devine:
Et souvent même il fait beaucoup
D'éviter sa ruine.
Plus d'un se perd, comme le Loup,
Par sa propre machine.

LE ROSSIGNOL ET L'AUTOUR
Fable XXI (Sur l'Air, "Ton humeur est Catereine")
(Ventre à jeun n'a point d'oreilles) (Ier Recueil, Air XIII — see p 58)
English summary on p. 175

I

Philomele* au beau langage,
Sous les serres de l'Autour**
Eut beau dire: Mon ramage
Des Rois mêmes est l'amour;
L'Autour dit: C'est leur affaire,
S'ils s'en veulent contenter,
Quant à moi, ce ne l'est guere
De t'entendre ici chanter.
*Rossignol   **Oiseau de proie

II

Tes grands auditeurs sans doute
A leur aise avoient diné:
Tu prétens que je t'écoute;
Et je n'ai pas déjeuné.
Ventre à jeun n'a point
    d'oreilles
Pour entendre une chanson:
Que lui servent les merveilles?
On ne dine pas de son.

III

Cela dit, il expédie
Sans quartier l'Oiseau chanteur.
Dequoi sert la mélodie,
Ou le ton doux et flateur?
Des mains d'un Tiran barbare
Qui cherche à vous dévorer,
L'éloquence la plus rare
Ne sauroit vous délivrer.

LE CIGNE, ET LE CUISINIER
Fable XXII (Sur l'Air, "Ton humeur est Catereine")
(Parole douce) (Ier Recueil, Air XIII — See p 58)
English summary on p. 175

I
Dans une ménagerie
Un Cigne avec un Oison
Habitoient de compagnie,
Et de pair à compagnon:
Le premier chantoit au Maître
Des chansons pleines d'appas.
Le second ne devoit être
Que pour servir au repas.

II
Mais par une erreur insigne,
L'officier ayant trop bu,
Pour l'Oison happa le Cigne:
Le Chanteur étoit perdu:
On l'alloit mettre en potage
Par bonheur il se plaignit.
Aux accens de son ramage
L'Homme fut tout interdit.

III
Va, dit-il, et me pardonne
De m'être à ce point mépris:
J'en veux à la gent Oisonne
Qui m'assomme par ses cris.
Apprens de cette avanture,
Et sans cesse t'en souvien,
Qu'en semblable conjoncture
Doux parler ne nuit de rien.

LE LOUP, ET LES BERGERS
Fable XXIII (sur le même Air)
(Le mauvais Exemple)
English summary on p. 175

I
Un Loup, comme le raconte
Un Auteur accrédité,
Eut un jour regret et honte
De son trop de cruauté.
Eh quoi! sur toute la terre,
Disoit-il, je suis haï;
Et pour me faire la guerre
Un chacun s'arme à l'envi.

II
D'où vient cette rage étrange
Qui sans cesse me poursuit?
De quelque Agneau que je
mange,
Ou quelque Chien mal instruit.
Tout cela vault-il la peine
D'être en butte à tant de traits?
Prevenons enfin la haine,
Et broutons dans les guerets.

III
Comme il parle, il voit tout proche
Par hazard dans un verger,
D'un Agneau cuit à la broche
Maint Titire* s'heberger:
Quoi! dit-il, je crains de faire
Ce que font ces Messieurs là?
Ce n'est donc pas grande affaire
De manger comme cela.
*Berger

IV
Je foudrai comme un Hercule
Sur les veaux et les moutons.
Et serois bien ridicule
De me réduire aux chardons:
Mon scrupule étoit folie,
De l'example je l'apprens:
Allons, ma premiere vie,
Sans tarder je vous reprens.

Bibliography

Anthony, James R. *French Baroque Music,* revised edition. New York: Norton, 1978.

Arger, Jane. *Les Agréments et le rythme.* Paris: Rouart, Lerolle et Cie., 1921. This book is based on on a survey of Bérard, Blanchet, Brossard, David, Lecuyer, and others.

Bacilly, Bénigne de. *Remarques curieuses sur l'art de bien chanter* (Paris: 1668) Translated by Austin B. Caswell. New York: The Institute of Mediaeval Music: 1968.

Bérard, Jean-Baptiste. *L'Art du chant.* Paris, 1755.

Batteaux, Charles. *Cours de belle-lettres,* 1763.

Blanchet, l'abbé Joseph. *Art ou principes philosophiques du chant*, Paris, 1756.

Brossard, Sébastien. *Dictionnaire de musique.* Paris, 1703

Capelle, Pierre Adolphe. *La Clé du Caveau.* Paris: l'Abel Lanoi, 1816.

Couperin, François, *Piéces de Clavecin.* Edited by Kenneth Gilbert. Paris: Heugel & Col., 1972

David, François. *Méthode nouvelle ou principes généraux pour apprendre facilement la musique et l'art de chanter.* Paris, 1737.

Dellain, Ch.-Henri. *Nouveau manuel musical contenant les éléments de la musique, des agréments, du chant.* Paris, l781.

l'abbé Demotz de la Salle. *Méthode de musique selon un nouveau système.* 1728.

Duckles, Vincent. Review of Bacilly. *M.L.S. Notes* XX1V/3 (March 1970) 527–28.

Folk-Lore and Fable—Aesop, Grimm, Anderson, from the *Harvard Classics.* Edited by Charles W. Eliot. New York: P.F. Collier & Son, 1937.

Keller, Hermann. *Thoroughbass Method.* New York: Norton 1965.

La Fontaine. Jean de. *Fables.* Paris: Garnier-Flammarion, 1966.

Lecuyer, *Principes de l'art du chant, suivant les règles de la langue et de la prosedie françoise.* Paris, 1769.

Mercure de France (Jan 1730) 114–19.

Montéclair, Michel Pignolet de. *Principes de musique, divisez en quatre partis.* Paris, 1736.

Morrissette, Bruce A. "La Fontaine." *Collier's Encyclopedia,* 24 vols. U.S.: Crowell-Collier Educational Corporation, 1969, XIV, 253.

Noel, Thomas. *Theories of the Fable in the Eighteenth Century.* New York & London: Columbia University Press, 1975.

Parfaict, Claude and Francois. *Dictionnaire des théâtres de Paris, 7 vols,* (Paris, 1756) Reprint of 1767-70 ed., Geneva, 1971.

Praetorius, Michael, *Syntagma musicum, Tomas tertius (1619)*. Edited and trans. by E. Bernouli. Leipzig, 1916.

Répertoire International des Sources Musicales. Published by the International Musicological Society and the International Association of Music Libraries, München-Duisburg: G. Henle, 1964, Vol. B 11.

Rockwell, John. Review of Dec. 18, 1979 recital by John Metz. *The New York Times* (Dec 23, 1979) 32.

Rousseau, Jean-Jacques. "Vaudeville." *Dictionnaire de Musique*. Paris, 1768, 531–32.

Sanford, Sally. "A Guide to Singing the French Language According to the Principles in Seventeenth-and Eighteenth-Century Treaties." Unpublished term project, Stanford University, 1979.

_____."Seventeenth and Eighteenth Century Vocal Style and Technique," Unpublished D.M.A. dissertation, Stanford University, 1979.

DICTIONARIES

Dictionnaire du français classique. by Jean Dubois, René Lagane, and Alain Lerond. Paris: Larousse, 1971.

Dictionnaire alphabétique & analgique de la langue Française. by Paul Robert Paris, 1970.

RECORDINGS

Corneille, Pierre. *Polyeucte—Tragedy in Five Acts*. Excerpts performed by the Comédie Française. Period Records FRL 1507.

"Songs from Shakespeare, Bach, and La Fontaine," performed by Hugues Cuenod, tenor, and Albert Fuller, harpsichord. Cambridge Records CRS 1702.

VII.

The English Summaries

The following summaries are included here in order to give the basic story of each fable. My intention is simply to prevent the reader from being frustrated by one hundred and twenty-seven stories in eighteenth-century French. Of course when preparing to perform the *Fables* one should make a complete word-for-word translation. In making a detailed translation, the following points may be helpful.

The largest single problem is that the *Fables* in the *Nouvelles Poésies* are abridged versions of La Fontaine. In some cases so much has been left out that one must go back to the original in order to understand the story. This was probably not a problem for eighteenth-century performers, as the La Fontaine *Fables* were well-known to them.

In doing the translations, one needs access to a variety of French dictionaries. I found two which were especially helpful: the *Petit Robert*, and the Larousse *Dictionnaire du Français Classique* (see bibliography).

If a word doesn't seem to appear in the dictionary, it may be that the spelling has changed since the eighteenth century. Try doubling a consonant that wasn't doubled in the text. Be alert for a missing letter, like the *p* in temps. Note that a tilde (~) was sometimes used to indicate nasalization (e.g., retõbent for retombent). With a little experimentation with spelling, one can find almost any word in a comprehensive dictionary.

VOLUME ONE

I. La Fourmi, et la Sauterelle/The Ant and the Grasshopper
    "Laziness"
During the summer the Grasshopper sang and bounded, being lazy. But prompt and faithful to her work, the Ant didn't do as *she* did. During the summer.
During the winter, the Grasshopper was without an allowance, and forced to live on air. So the Ant in her abundance told her, "Now sing!" During the winter.

II. Le Corbeau et le Renard/The Crow and the Fox
        "Flattery"

The Crow holds the cheese, the Fox is drawn by the smell. The Fox flatters the Bird, who crows with pleasure. The Fox gets the cheese, and advises the Crow that one never flatters another for naught. *The admirer only admires you in order to get your goods.*

III. Le Conseil des Rats/The Rats' Council
        "The Little Bell"

The rat people decided to hang a little bell around the Cat's neck, so as to know his every move. But when it came to actually volunteering to do it, not one Rat came forth. *When one deliberates, there is plenty of courage, but when the time comes for action, all is repugnance and cowardice.*

IV. Le Rat dans un fromage de Hollande/The Rat in the Holland Cheese
        "The Hypocrite Recluse"

In his cheese lived a Rat, like a monk — never fearing the Cat, and rarely associating with others. Does this remind you of anyone? I say that all hermits are hypocrites when devoid of charity. When they vaunt their austerity, then their misanthropy is no saintliness — no matter how much they pray and meditate.

V.   Le Chien qui se voit dans l'eau/The Dog who saw Himself in the Water
        "The Shadow Mistaken for Reality"

The clear water mirrored back the dainty morcel that the dog held in his mouth. So he dropped what he had in order to get what he saw. *For a wish or an illusion, greed loses all sense of reality. Such is the human sickness.*

VI. Le Loup et l'Agneau/The Wolf and the Lamb
        "Oppression"

A Wolf, higher upstream from the Lamb, said, "You are troubling my water." The Lamb replied, "Notice, Mister, that it descends from you to me." The Wolf, "This past year you've been against me." The Lamb, "How so, I wasn't even born." The Wolf, "Then it must have been your brother." The Lamb, "I haven't any."

The Wolf then ate the Lamb. *The innocent one cries out in vain for justice, when injustice and force are banded against her.*

VII. La Genisse, la Chévre, la Brebis, et le Lion/The Heifer, the Goat, the Ewe, and the Lion
        "Might makes Right"

Don't associate yourself with those who are too big for you. When the mother Ewe joined the Heifer, the Goat and the Lion on a hunt, it was a vain thing to do. For when the Stag was taken, the Lion justified having all the portions for himself.

VIII. Les deux Chévres/The Two Goats
        "A Point of Honor"

A haughty Goat, on a small bridge, found himself faced with another, no less proud. "Yield me passage." "I don't want to." In this dispute Goats provoke one another, and in pushing, somersault into the water. *How many of us are equally foolish?*

IX. La Lice et sa Compagne/The Big Dog and His Consort
        "Ingratitude"

Once upon a time a large Dog loaned his bed and fireside to a neighborly Bitch so she could have her litter. She continually postponed letting him return, until finally the Pups were large enough to force him to stay away. *Don't loan things to evil persons. They'll trifle with you, and make you plead. Yours is a lost cause.*

X.   La Chévre le Chevreau et le Loup/The Goat, the Kid, and the Wolf
        "Mistrust"

"Don't open the door unless you hear this password: 'Foin du Loup et de sa race,' " said the Goat to the Kid. The Wolf, passing by, heard this and remembered it. When the Mother was away, he disguised his voice and gave the password. The Kid insisted on seeing a white paw in addition to hearing the password. *Admire the Mother's foresight, but even more the Kid's caution.*

XI.   Le Renard, et le Loup/The Fox and the Wolf
        "Taken in"

A Fox let himself fall into the bottom of a well. (After all, no one walks perfectly, and even Alexander's horse stumbled once in awhile.) He faked a good laugh, and convinced the Wolf to join him, pointing out the quality of the cheese in the bottom of the well. If the Wolf would get into one bucket, the Fox could come out in the other bucket, due to the Wolf's weight. What was the cheese? The moon's image in the water!

XII.   L'Ane portant une Idole/The Donkey Carrying an Idol
        "Foolish Dignity"

A Donkey carried on his back a false God, which people adored, and he took for himself all the homage that everyone paid to the idol. *It is thus that a fool vainly imagines that people render to him the homage which are actually directed at the trappings of dignity.*

XIII.   La Montagne en travail/The Mountain in Labor
        "Lots of Noise, Small Effect"

Once upon a time the whole countryside shuddered, as a certain mountain was giving forth in childbirth. From the great cries, one would have thought a whole town was being born. But only a Mouse came forth. *People always vaunt themselves, and promise with great pomp. But often they bear nothing more valuable than our Rat.*

XIV.   L'Antre du Lion/The Lion's Den
        "Prudence"

When the King of Animals was ill, no one could persuade any of his woodland people to visit him. They were shown all sorts of passports, and given assurances. The Fox noted that there were hundreds of paths leading into the Lion's den, but asked, "How does one get out of there?"

XV.   La Perdrix et le Levraut/The Partridge and the Young Hare
        "The Insulter Punished"

Guard against insulting those who are in pain, for when your turn comes people will say you deserved it. They tell of a young Hare in agony, in the teeth of a Dog, Miraut. A Partridge scorned the Hare, noting that while the Hare had speed, Miraut had both that and power. But a Goshawk heard this, and proved his own superior speed and strength.

XVI.   Le Héron/The Heron
        "Scorn"

'Tis the scorn of Heron of which I sing. Tench and Carp showed themselves in schools under the Heron's eyes, but he disdained them, saying, "I can do better to wait." But when the fish disappeared, leaving him only a slug to eat, he lamented. Meanwhile the Magpie ceaselessly repeated, "You fool, you fool, you fool."

XVII.   Les deux Mulets/The Two He-Mules
        "Dangerous Pomp"

Two Mules took a voyage, the one loaded with gold, the other with garden fruits. The first went off conceitedly, leaving the other behind, like a cad. A thief, drawn by the noise of the first Mule's bell, attacked and beat him. The other Mule shook his head saying, "Dear Comrade, I esteem your employment, but I'd rather carry the salad — You see why."

XVIII. La Grenouille et le Boeuf/The Frog and the Ox
        "Ambition"

Good sense says that everyone should remain in his own sphere. Evil will come to those who are impractical. An ambitious Frog puffed herself up in order to equal the monstrous size of an Ox. But she was so puffed up with her project that she burst.

XIX.   Le Renard et les Raisins/The Fox and the Grapes
        "Braggadocio"

A certain Fox, a braggard, saw one day on a trellis some beautiful green grapes, which promised a delicate feast. He tried to jump for them, but the prey was too high. "I'd be naive to try again; They're only sour grapes—fit for common folk. I'll let someone else take them."

XX.   La Bélette dans le grenier/The Weasel in the Granary
        "Trapped Thieves"

A skinny Weasel entered a granary last winter, through a small hole. She made a good living there, and grew fat. Now her stomach was so stretched that she couldn't leave. *Many thieves slip into the business of a Lord, but are unable to leave.*

XXI.   La Lionne et L'Ourse/Mrs. Lion and Mrs. Bear
        "Unaware of Another's Misfortune"

Mrs. Lion had a son who was snared one day in a trap. Uproar! Uproar! The Queen Mother roared so much that the whole countryside was in alarm. "All the children," said Mrs. Bear, "alas, who have died from your efforts of late—do you think they died having neither father nor mother?" "No," replied the other, "but other's misfortunes never bother my soul." And Mrs. Bear replied, "Too bad, Madame."

XXII.   Le Cerf se mirant dans l'eau/The Deer at the Water Hole
        "Usefulness and Beauty"

A young Deer was admiring himself in a clear fountain, being not impressed by his legs, but by his antlers. Suddenly he leapt when he heard a Lion approaching, and he ran quickly until his antlers got caught in some branches. As he was about to be killed he sighed, "The beauty that pleases us, and the good that bores us—the one brings fortune, the other proves fatal. I despised that which saves my life....Alas, I loved that which only brings trouble."

XXIII. Le Coq et le Renard/The Rooster and the Fox
        "Cunning meets its Match"

A Rooster was on pre-dawn guard duty when a Fox called on him to trick him, saying, "Peace is made, universal friendships. I'm delegated to make the treaty." The Bird, who wasn't stupid, replied, "By my comb, I'll agree. But don't I see two Dogs running towards us, and jumping over the furrows like messengers?" "There is general peace, and a Congress," said the Fox scurrying away to the fields, "but I have business to take care of." The Rooster laughed, and told the Hens and Capons of the adventure. They repeated and clamored of it, with no little honor for he who outfoxed the Fox.

XXIV.   Les Oreilles du Lièvre/The Ears of the Hare
        "Fear"

A stranger gored the Lion, who then declared that all horned ones would be exiled from his domain. When the Hare heard this he said, "Ah! I am banished, for I have two such horns." In vain others told him that they were just ears, but he replied, "At the mercy of jealous ones, ears become horns." *It is thus when one is afraid. All things are transformed—a thicket is a thief, a ghost, or terrible thing.*

XXV.   Le Lion et L'Ane à la chasse/The Lion and the Donkey at the Hunt
        "Impressive Airs"

A Lion, who was a strong hunter, went hunting with a Jackass which had a stentorian voice that imitated hunting horns so well that it was butchery all day long. The braying Ass claimed all the honor, even from the Lion. *If one condemns important airs, who would tol-*

erate such an Ass? But we know that men of no substance are like that. Let them be, without quarreling.

XXVI. Les Membres et l'Estomac/The Limbs and the Stomach
  "Disagreement"

The limbs conspired, and declared to the stomach that they were tired of caring for this Monsieur, and persisted on this basis. The fruit of this mutiny was that the blood no longer travelled, and the humours which give life shortly vanished. Because of this experience, all returned and intelligence was again maintained. Henceforth no malcontents or loiterers. *Happy is the state which works that way.*

VOLUME TWO

I. L'Hirondelle, et les Petits Oiseaux/The Swallow and the Little Birds
  "Intractability"

The Swallow told the little Birds that the flax they see may be woven into snares to trap them. Though they laughed at her, it all came to pass. The youngest Birds went into the stew; the best Birds were put into cages to sing. *You may preach uselessly, but it comes to pass, as it did in Cassandra's time, that the listener comes to feel a useless repentance.*

II. L'Ours et les deux Gascons/Mrs. Bear and the Two Braggarts
  "The Bear's Hide"

Two broke braggarts got the idea of stealing a hide which they planned to take from a vagrant Bear. But when they came upon the Bear, their hair stood straight on end with fear. One escaped by climbing a tree; the other feigned death. Mrs. Bear sniffed around him, and her expression seemed to say, "Don't put a price on *my* hide 'til you've taken it."

III. La Chévre, le Mouton, et le Cochon gras/The Nanny-Goat, the Ram, and the Fat Pig
  "Useless Laments"

Mrs. Goat and Mr. Ram went together with a fat Pig to the fair, but neither to steal nor to watch the charlatan Tabarin doing his trick — for only humans do that. Far from laughing, the Swine sighed and cried, as he could imagine himself under the knife. But the others said nothing, and I believe they did well thereby. *When you can't avoid pain, what good does it do to lament?*

IV. Le Renard et le Bouc/The Fox and the He-Goat
  "Foresight"

The refined Fox and the not-too-bright He-Goat took a trip together. Thirst overtook them, but when they found a well the problem was not how to get into it, but how to get out. The cunning Fox suggested that he could climb up on the Goat's horns, and then hoist the Goat up. The Goat thought this was a wonderful idea. But the Fox climbed out, left him in disgrace, and lectured him on his lack of foresight.

V. Le Frommage/The Cheese
  "A Rage of Pleading"

We sing this song in an entertaining key. It's a question of some good cheese which was seized by two tomcats. To divide it up Bertrand the Monkey was called. He asked for a scale, in order to be legal about it. He devoured the surplus from one side and then the other. What remained went "for judge's fees." Though people laughed on all sides, it is still true that *we don't know how to live without legal process.*

VI. Le Geai, paré des plumes du Paon/The Jay Adorned in Peacock Feathers
  "Ridiculous Vanity"

"Keep to your suitable garb, village Jay. Leave to the Peacocks their beautiful plumage and the allure of the château." But it got into his head that he could really glitter by taking the molted plumage of a Peacock and parading in it. But the Peacocks pecked the plumage off him. Then he fled in tatters to his family, which hooted at him and saluted him with sarcasm.

VII.   Le Rat et l'Huître/The Rat and the Oyster
"The Ninny"

A Rat left his cave in order to see the world. He was transported with joy when he came upon the ocean. He didn't even know what a ship was when he saw one. Coming upon an Oyster, he decided to eat it. When he stretched his neck out and into the Oyster, it defended itself by closing upon him. *Thus what he thought he'd take took him!*

VIII.   Le Meunier, son Fils, et l'Ane/The Miller, his Son, and the Ass
"You can't please everyone"

A miller and his son were carrying their Donkey suspended between them, in order that it would be plump and fresh to sell at the fair. The first who saw them jested at them, and convinced them to ride the Ass. Others said it was not strong enough for two, so the father got off, leaving the son on. Others thought the son should walk, letting the father ride. Finally the father decided to consult himself, saying, *"When can one do what everyone else wants him to do? Never!"*

IX.   L'Homme, la Citrouille, et le Gland/The Man, the Pumpkin, and the Acorn
"Providence"

Let us admire Providence, and be less critical of it. "This stalk is too small for the gourd which is growing from it. It would be better to hang it from one of those oaks so as to see it better." But while our fool was thinking that, an acorn fell on his head. "Let's leave the gourd and the acorn in their places," he said. "If the gourd had fallen on me I would have been pulverized."

X.   Le Renard, et le Buste/The Fox and the Bust
"Vain Semblance"

They tell us that in days of yore a bronze-caster put on view in his shop a portrait of a certain warrior. Everyone admired it, but the Fox mingled in with the crowd and said, "Yes the head is beautiful, but it has a flaw—no brains."

XI.   Le Statuaire/The Sculptor
"Illusion"

A sculptor bought a beautiful block of marble, and pondered whether it should become a God, a table, or a basin. "It will become God," he said. His craft was so good in making this thundering idol, that one thought the only thing missing from his Jupiter was speech. *Everyone turns his dreams into reality, and gets seduced by self-created falsehood.*

XII.   L'Huître, et les Plaideurs/The Oyster and the Litigants
"The Trial"

One day two travellers came across an Oyster. They went to the law to see who would get it. Master Dadin, the judge, opened the Oyster and ate it. That, poor suitor, is the end of your long legal battles. *The Senator gets the Oyster. You get the shells.*

XIII.   Le Rat, et l'Eléphant/The Rat and the Elephant
"Foolish Vanity"

A Rat next to an enormous Elephant said, "A Rat is worth as much in its little body. 'Tis not important who takes up more or less space. I'm more graceful." As he said this, a Cat came and mocked him, saying, "A Rat is no Elephant," and ate him. *This Rat is a constant image of human self-conceit.*

XIV.   L'Ane, vêtu de la peau du Lion/The Ass, Dressed in a Lion's Hide
"Fanfare"

The Ass seemed formidable under the Lion's hide—until someone got his name, at which time the contemptible beast was seen as a mere braggart, a true Ass. *More than one has proclaimed himself Hero in vain language, and after this introduction appears in the Ass's image.*

XV.   Le Rat de ville et le Rat des champs/The City Rat and the Country Rat
        "Country living"

One evening the Country Rat paid the City Rat a visit, and ate luxuriously. A sad mishap spoiled the affair when some Cats arrived. "Adieu," said the Country Rat. "Never in the deepest woods have I so trembled. I'll leave you your Kings and your fears."

XVI.   La Tortue, et les deux Canards/The Turtle and the Two Ducks
        "Imprudent Babble, and Vain Curiosity"

A harebrained Turtle wanted to travel. So two Ducks suspended between them a stick which the pilgrim-Turtle could hang onto by his teeth. The Birds carried her through the clouds to everyone's astonishment. When the crowds hailed the Queen of the Turtles, she claimed to be just that. In doing so however, she let go of the baton and fell. Others laughed, but she cried.

XVII.   Les Poissons, et le Cormoran/The Fish and the Cormorant
        "Foolish Reliance"

Who would think that the aquatic people would let themselves be taken in by a Cormorant. But when a fisherman came the Bird offered them his place for refuge, then ate them. *The Fish is a foolish breed, but people are equally so.*

XVIII. Le Pêcheur, et le Petit Poisson/The Fisherman and the Little Fish
        "Profit from the Present"

Little Fish become large ones, God willing. But I hold that it's foolishness to wait for that. My proverb is: *A little Fish in your sack is worth more than a great Pike still swimming.*

XIX.   La jeune Dogue, et sa Mere/The Young Mastiff and his Mother
        "Useful Loss"

A Young Dog lamented when his master cut off his ears, and put a large collar around him. But his mother reminded him that it was for his own good—that in order not to risk anything from the Wolves, one must wear iron collars, and have no ears.

XX.   Le Renard, et le Chat/The Fox and the Cat
        "Resources"

Mr. Fox applauded himself for his finesse, and said to Mr. Rodillard (a Cat), "No Cat can equal Mr. Fox. I have a thousand tricks to save me from misfortune." Mr Tomcat said, "I have one trick, and am content with it. I know how to climb." *You only need one resource, if it is good enough.*

XXI.   L'Ane, et le petit Chien/The Ass the the Small Dog
        "Clumsy"

An Ass pointed out a little Doggy, which was the companion of a couple, and he decided to imitate the Dog. So, he came to his Master's armchair with a foot all covered with mud, and sang a song. "Oh, what beautiful melody and playing," said the Master. "But to finish the comedy you must dance." No matter how he tried, the clumsy one made but a poor attempt. *You'll never be graceful if you force your talent.*

XXII.   Le Louvat, et le Cheval/The Young Wolf and the Horse
        "Indescretion"

A young greenhorn Wolf, who had never seen anything, found a great king of a Stud Horse on his doorstep. He said to him, "Beau Sire, What is your name?" The other replied, "You'd know it if you knew how to read, for it's written on my bridle." The fool approached, ogling as best he could. Mr. Horse let him have it between the eyes with his iron hoof, and sent him away looking for his comrades, far from the Stud Horses.

XXIII.   L'Aigle, et le Corbeau/The Eagle and the Crow
        "Dangerous Example"
Example is a bait which can fool people, for without genius or force one is left with shame when trying to follow an example above one's head. An Eagle is always an Eagle; a Crow is always a Crow. This smart rule displeased the black Bird who decided to imitate the Eagle in stealing mutton. After a struggle, the Crow's feet were well tangled in wool. Along came the Master, who gave him over to his Dog.

XXIV.   La Poule aux Oeufs d'Or/The Hen with the Golden Eggs
        "Greed"
The Hen which laid golden eggs each day was a treasure to its Master. But he capriciously decided to have the whole treasure at once, thinking himself clever. He was only an idiot, thinking he had the whole portion in the Hen's belly. He disembowelled her, found nothing, and put her into the stew. Did she lay eggs anymore?

VOLUME THREE

I.   La Besace/Beggary
        "Self-love"
Each has his advantages and faults. Among the animal kingdom each one thinks he is the best. Once when the animals had meetings, the Monkey praised himself, and booed the Bear. The Bear, being content with its shape, made faces at the Elephant for its size. The Elephant in turn criticised both the Whale and the Ant. *We are all the poorer for our self-love.*

II.   L'Ane, et le Chien/The Ass and the Dog
        "Mutual Aid"
We must help one another, for even the strongest yields without assistance. But to ever be helped, one must give help also. The silly Ass defied this moral when he gave not a bit of food to his friend, the hungry Dog. Later, when his Master was asleep, the bloodthirsty Wolf came. Though he brayed his best, the Dog did not come to the Ass's aid. The Wolf was too strong, and tore the Ass to pieces.

III.   Le Singe Adopté/The Adopted Monkey
        "The Native"
A foolish man decided that since he had no children, he would adopt the Monkey Bertrand for his own. There was Monsieur Monkey richly adorned — with diamonds, blond wig, etc. — the new Adonis. He had teachers of all sorts, and took on the customs of a millionaire. But with age one reaches his majority. Bertrand, without a page boy or a governor, tumbled and became deranged. He took to climbing the rooftops. *A metamorphosis in temperament is never easily achieved.*

IV.   Le Satire, et son Hôte/The Satyr and his Guest
        "Duplicity"
Seated at the dinner table, the Satyr saw his guest breathing sometimes on his hands (to warm them) and sometimes on his food (to cool it). "Why this?" he asked. The guest explained, and the Sylvan Beast threw him out. "Go," he said, "Do your puffing in Normandy — you who blow both hot and cold with the same breath."

V.   L'Astrologue, Qui se laisse tomber dans un puits/The Astrologer, who let Himself
        Fall into a Well
        "The Vanity of Astrology"
One who was clever with the horoscope, and who pretended to read the skies, was walking

along with a long telescope so that he could watch some planets. There appeared a well beneath his feet, and the false prophet fell in. As we say, ladies and gentlemen have the folly to consult charlatans. *Astrology and magic are equally foolish.*

VI.   Le Lièvre, et les Grenouilles/The Hare and the Frogs
      "Fear"

"Ah!" cried the Hare at his lodging. "How fear makes one unhappy. The slightest agitation sends the timid running." Even the sound of the wind sent him running, as he thought it was hunting horns. Our chicken-hearted fellow found even more timid ones in his flight, including some Frogs which leapt into their pond when he approached. He knew that he had to have courage, even though he belonged to a fearful race.

VII. La Vieille, et les deux Servantes/The Old Woman and the Two Servants
      "From Bad to Worse"

The two servants were discontented at the old woman's house, and not without reason. Always spinning, always in her room playing cards, and up at the Cock's crow — even in December. "Evil Cock," they said, "You'll die." But things only got worse after they killed the Bird. All night in her lodging, worrying and on the watch, she demanded to know the hour. They used to be able to close their eyes, and were better off before the Cock died.

VIII. Les deux Chiens/The Two Dogs
      "Inclination"

We sing the story of two Dogs — the one accomplished great works, subduing many Hares, and covering himself with glory. The other was truly lazy, drunken, and a glutton — always sleeping and eating, and thus called "Laridon." Here and in Royalty it's the same: Of the two brothers the one acquires honor, the other — nothing. He is only a Laridon. (Note: "Laridon" appears in none of the dictionaries. Possibly *lardon* is meant, which is a slice of bacon. Also, *lardonner* is to taunt.)

IX.   Le Singe, et le Léopard/The Monkey and the Leopard
      "Diversity"

Gille the Monkey, along with the less refined Leopard, made posters to advertise their arts to the village dolts. The Leopard said, "Come, Messieurs, to see the miracle of my colors. They are like inlaid floors." Gille said, "I promise perilous jumps, ingenious tricks, etc." The Monkey knew people well, for they left after seeing the medley of colors. *Wit is better than clothing.*

X.   Le Savetier enrichi/The Rich Cobbler
      "Uneasiness of Riches"

A Cobbler sang and laughed in his poverty. But when opulence came his way — good-by song and peaceful repose. Since then, he fears theft, jumps at the slightest noise, and never sleeps. *Money is no blessing. He who seeks riches seeks anxiety.*

XI.   Le Loup plaidant contre le Renard, par-devant le Singe/Fox Against Wolf
      "The Monkey's Judgement"

We sing of the Monkey's judgement. His equitable decision was subtle, and at first the truth seems to contradict it. The Wolf was brought to justice by a clever Fox, without proof. He defended himself, and denied having taken anything. The judge, knowing well their natures, convicted both of them — the one for black machinations, the other for robbery.

XII. Les deux Voleurs, et l'Ane/The Two Thieves and the Ass
      "Fishing in Troubled Water"

An Ass was stolen by two rogues. Each one wanted it, and that led to a great quarrel. When a third robber arrived, he mounted the Ass, and spurred it away. The others, to their shame, were fighting for naught. *Better to have agreement than this strange competition.*

XIII.   Le Païsan, et l'Ours/The Peasant and the Bear
"The Obliging Fool"

Don't be social with rough friends, for even their goodness can do you harm. Once upon a time a man had a Bear for his companion. While the man slept, a Flea jumped onto his nose. So his foolish friend hit him on the mouth with a brick. He had good intentions, but was only a beast who thought to help his friend.

VOLUME FOUR

I.   Le Combat des Bélettes, et des Rats/The War between the Weasels and the Rats
"Dangerous Pomp"

Let us sing of war and combat—but not of heros in Homer, but of the Weasels and the Rats. They were fighting in the trenches, with rage in their faces. Thousands of fighters had fallen on the plains. Finally the Rats had to flee; their remaining soldiers had to hide. But these soldiers had decided to wear great plumages on their helmets. Because of this they could not hide, and there was a great carnage. *Thus pretention is like an ephemeral gust of wind, which sinks the great.*

II.   La Bélette, et le Lapin/The Weasel and the Rabbit
"The Sycophant"

One day a Rabbit was in court with a Weasel. Mr. Mouse-eater (the Cat) was the judge, assuming gentle manners. He ended their differences by eating them. *I have respect for those who give audiences, but my suspicion of them makes me flee —above all from the language of a wheedling swindler.*

III.   Le Chat, et le vieux Rat/The Cat and the Old Rat
"Precaution"

The Cat had a new invention for trapping Mice. He suspended himself up high, so that he looked like he had been hanged. So the Mice came out of their attic—no longer confining themselves. Then the hanged one resuscitated himself and jumped on them. "We know there are others," he said, "We'll get them sooner or later." Then he took flour and made himself an overcoat of it, and got into an open trough. The Rats then came sniffing. But an old Rat saw the ruse—that it was neither bran nor flour. "It's the Cat!" he said. *At the least suspicion, mistrust is a good thing, in order to not be surprised.*

IV.   L'Enfant, et le Maître d'Ecole/The Child and the Schoolmaster
"The Pedant"

Harangue after harangue—What good does it do? "Pedant, restrain your language, and come to my help. Come quickly and hold me up," said a young student about to drown. Meanwhile the Teacher continued with new sermons.

V.   Le Pot de Terre, et le Pot de Fer/The Earthen Pot and the Iron Pot
"Temerity"

Why expose yourself to the risk of a storm? A clay pitcher is easily cracked when collided against a bronze one, and is broken. *One says it was well-deserved foolishness.*

VI.   Le Lion et le Moucheron/The Lion and the Gnat
"Arrogance"

The little ones often do terrible things to the big ones. A vile Gnat pestered and stung a Lion, with a bite one could hardly see. But the Master was greatly in error, and everyone blamed him for having aggravated, scolded, and menaced the insect. Ah! He was paid back for his uncivilized arrogance.

VII.   Le Lion, et le Rat/The Lion and the Rat
      "Humanity"

When a Rat found himself under the Lion's paw, the proud animal did him no harm. Far from being angry, he gave him his life and was tender to him. Some days later, the Lion was caught in a trap. Our Rat was neither ungrateful nor useless. He came quickly and gnawed the cords of the trap. As the old fables say, *Little people can be of help to great people.*

VIII. Le Paon et le Rossignol/The Peacock and the Nightingale
      "Envy"

"There's nothing in nature which doesn't sing better than I do," said the Peacock. "Why do I know less than the Nightingale about sharps and flats?" Philomèle (the Nightingale) in her language replied, "What are you saying, don't you have the most beautiful plumage — and still you are envious?"

IX.   Le Renard, et le Lion/The Fox and the Lion
      "Habit"

It happened that a Fox found himself at the Lion's place. Having never seen him before, the Fox was seized with horror, and swooned with fear. The good Lion told his pages to bring the Fox back to him that evening after having restored him (when he was feeling better). At the second meeting, the Fox was afraid, but not so much dismayed. "Bring him again tomorrow," said the Sovereign. Finally he became a familiar of the Monarch. *By long habit, fear, hate, and repugnance can be overcome. But one may come by this means to evil as well as to good.*

X.   La Cour de Lion/The Lion's Court
      "The Refined Courtesan"

The Sultan Lion filled his palace with all his subjects, in order to know over whom he was ruler. But the Bear held his nose — the smell was so bad. The King, in anger, asked the Monkey what he thought. The Monkey praised the odor — which didn't please the King any better. Like a true Caligula, he strangled him. But the Fox, when asked what he thought, said, "Unfortunately, I have a cold." *I think it is better to neither flatter nor to speak sincerely with noblemen.*

XI.   La Mouche, et le Coche/The Fly and the Coach
      "Vain Eagerness"

A chariot was stuck in a thick bog, the axle sunk along with the wheel. And the driver was crying out in rage when a Fly approached. "Let's get the coach going," she said, flying about, turning, and always humming. The horses were worn out, but the Fly pursued, needling them first on the flank, then on the nape of the neck. She spoke poorly of this dawdling. Finally they got out, and the impertinent one took all the honor. She even wanted payment for her great labor. *So it is in the human race! People who are forward, people who obstruct us, are people to chase away.*

XII. L'Aigle, la Corneille, et la Tortue/The Eagle, the Crow, and the Turtle
      "Wicked Counsel"

The Eagle had taken a Turtle, and intended to eat it. But it was out of danger — dressed in its shell. As much as he tried, his iron beak couldn't pierce the shell. An evil Crow (wanting a share of the spoils) advised that the Eagle drop the Turtle from a great height onto a dry rock. The Turtle did fall, and broke its roof, leaving the flesh no longer covered. *Force kills us less often than evil advice.*

XIII. Le Mulet entêté de sa Noblesse/The He-Mule, Intoxicated with his Nobility
      "It's an Ill Wind that Blows no Good"

A certain He-Mule was more taken with his nobility than a Paladin. He talked of his ancestors incessantly. He would not deign to serve even the smartest Doctors. Later on, he was confined to working at the mill, carrying flour. Then he remembered that his father also had carried flour. *Often enough, our misfortune is good for something, for it brings a pretentious person back to reason.*

XIV.   Le Lion s'en allant en Guerre/The Lion preparing for War
   "Everything serves its purpose"

When the Lion was preparing for war, he assigned duties to the animals according to their abilities. But a question arose as to what the stupid Donkey and the fearful Rabbit could do. But the King made the Rabbit his runner, and the Donkey his trumpet. *In the hands of able people nothing is useless — everything serves its purpose.*

XV.   Le Chêne, et le Roseau/The Oak and the Willow
   "By Request — at just the Moment"

The Oak tree noted that the Willow bends under the slightest sparrow, and bragged that it was stronger. But at just that moment, the North Wind slaughtered the Oak with a great noise, while the Willow only bent. *Don't be obstinate when it would be better to give a little. Vain effort is weakness.*

XIV.   L'Ane chargé de sel, et l'Ane chargé d'éponges/The Ass bearing salt, the Ass bearing sponges
   "Dangerous Imitation"

Two Asses found on their route a deep trench full of water. When the first went through, the salt he was carrying melted, and he went on. The second one, believing that he was without danger, and could also relieve himself of his burden, also plunged into the water without hesitating. But he didn't succeed so well. *The same path doesn't come out equally well for all.*

XVII.   Le Loup Berger/The Wolf-Shepherd
   "The Deceiver caught in his Trap"

He who wishes to deceive others often deceives himself. The Wolf dressed himself in a peasant shirt in order to take some Sheep. But the fool made his mistake when he called out to the Sheep to attract them, by offering them some food. The Sheep had taken him for the Shepherd until they heard his voice. At that point the Wolf was trapped by his own garments.

XVIII.   L'Araignée et la Goute/The Spider and the Gout
   "Each in his Own Place"

The Spider left his gilded and vaulted home, because everyone chased him all the time with a broom. The Gout [the disease often associated in earlier times with rich people], on the other hand, lived with a poor man, and was happy to trade. Thus they made their strange trade — with the Gout better off in a lord's house and the Spider in a grange.

XIX.   La Cierge/The Candle
   "Ignorance"

Be aware of your logic as well as your physical properties. A Candle believed it could outlast the fire, just as a flint does. So, out of ignorance, it threw itself into the flame and melted. What good did it do to know about the flint, and not know its own physical properties?

XX.   Mot de Socrate/The Words of Socrates
   "Rare good Friends"

Socrates had a modest house built for his own use — with no columns or porticos — all for commodity, not vanity. Most people found it too small, and criticized it. "Thanks to Heaven," said the Sage, "it is small enough for only true friends."

XXI.   Le Lion terrassé en peinture/The Lion knocked flat in a painting
   "People who make Fanfare"

They revealed a painting in which the artist had shown a Lion laid flat by one man. The spectators liked it, and praised the deed. A Lion which passed by put down their babble.

"Art and freedom to pretend have confused you. If a Lion had painted it, he would not have been the one to be beaten."

XXII.   Le Serpent, et le Villageois/The Serpent, and the Village Man
         "Ingratitude"

Is it good to be charitable? A village man took in a Serpent which was half-dead. But to reward him for it, the Snake attacked him. So the man cut off its head. *This is a good lesson for ungrateful people.*

VOLUME FIVE

I.   Le Vieillard, et ses Enfans/The Old Man and his Children
         "Concord"

An Old Man on his deathbed showed his wisdom to his children. He summoned them, and showed them thirty sticks he had bound together with cord. He challenged each of them to break the sticks, but they couldn't. *His advice to them was to stay together for strength.*

II.   Le Cheval, le Cerf, et l'Homme/The Horse, the Deer, and the Man
         "The Remedy is worse than the Sickness"

The Horse was broken, and regretted losing his liberty. It had been a losing battle against the fast-running Deer for rights at the watering hole, so the Horse had come to man for help — only to be mounted and bridled in exchange.

III.   Les deux Chiens, et leur Maître/The two Dogs and their Master
         "Education"

A certain rich Man had a little Dog who was lazy and only knew how to accompany his Master into town. His other Dog lacked nothing — neither ardor nor cleverness — so that when he went hunting he always brought back game. But the lazy Dog always got to taste the game at the Master's table, while the hunting Dog got stale bread thrown out the window, and was unhappy. The lazy Dog blamed the Master for training him to get by without work. *When one reproaches young people for being lazy, the criticism addresses itself to their parents.*

IV.   Le Chauve-Souris, et les deux Bélettes/The Bat and the two Weasels
         "Duplicity"

From her slum-lodging a foolish Bat went to take lodging with a Weasel, who thought of Rats as enemies. When the Weasel questioned the Bat about being possibly a Rat, the Bat claimed not to be a Rat, as he had wings. Then the Bat visited another Weasel who hated Birds. When this Weasel questioned that the Bat was a Bird, the Bat claimed to be a Rat — having fur. Eventually the Bat had its tongue cut out. *It is in vain that you lie, for others will have vengeance.*

V.   Le Souriceau, et sa Mere/The Baby Mouse, and its Mother
         "Looks can fool you"

The baby Mouse found the Cat attractive, and said that he found him tranquil and sweet. Yet he discovered that he trembled in the presence of the Rooster. His mother told him however, to leave the Cat alone, as he has nothing to eat at his table if not Rats, while the Rats often get nothing to dine on but Rooster. *Never judge by appearance.*

VI.   Le Cerf, et la Brebis/The Deer and the Sheep
         "Caution subjected to caution"

The Deer wanted to borrow a double measure of grain from the Sheep. He offered as reference the Wolf. The Sheep sniffed out a trap in this. With a Wolf as reference, the Deer hardly seemed like someone who would pay back the loan on time.

VII.   L'Ane, et ses Maîtres/The Donkey and his Masters
         "Love of Change"

"Always before dawn I have to get up to carry things," said the Donkey to the Gardener one day. "Such misfortune destiny gave me." So destiny gave him another fortune — to work for a Tanner. "Oh! How bad the skins smell, and I have to tremble under their weight. Gardener, how I wish I were back with you, where I could at least eat some cabbage by just turning my head." So fortune gave the Donkey a coal merchant for Master. *You're always changing, and never content.*

VIII.   L'Aigle, et le Renard/The Eagle and the Fox
         "No Enemies"

The Eagle took the Fox's offspring, who begged for their return. The Eagle was not touched by the Fox's prayers, and laughed from the top of his pine tree. "Don't I have some means?" asked the Fox. He went to a nearby temple, took a burning torch, and lit the tree. The Eagle happily returned the Fox's family to him, and made peace. *However big you are, take care not to offend the little ones, because they too are capable of vengeance.*

IX.   La Tortue, et l'Aigle/The Turtle and the Eagle
         "Opinionated Vanity"

The Turtle wanted to learn how to fly, and took lessons from the Eagle. The Eagle tried to discourage this dangerous plan, but got tired of the Turtle's entreaty. So he took her into the air, saying, "Put yourself on my back." Then he left her high on a mountain, to see how well she could fly. *I have seen many such a rascal climb up, only to fall down.*

X.   Le Lion, et la Grenouille/The Lion and the Frog
         "The Clamorer"

The King of the Forests heard such noises coming from a swamp, and wondered what they were. "Are they some giants or dragons? Could they make a Lion afraid?" So even though he was brave, he still had some fear. He advanced, roaring, and came upon a Frog, who was making all the racket. At first the Lion laughed, then blushed, then (chagrined by having been surprised by this noise) he crushed the beast. *Amongst humans you can find similarly vain persons, who from afar seem to be giants, but who are only dwarfs from near. One may think it's a Doctor, but it's only a clamorer.*

XI.   Les Oisons, et les Pigeons/The Goslings and the Pigeons
         "To the Rich, the Thieves"

Some fat Goslings passed some skinny Pigeons in the furrows, and came upon a troop of thieves. The Pigeons were able to fly away, while the Goslings were taken prey. *When the enemy takes a country that they have conquered, who risks the most — the great or the small? The great are the Goslings, and the small are the Pigeons.*

XII.   La Mouche, et la Fourmi/The Fly and the Ant
         "Stupid Vanity"

The Fly said, "I am at the King's table. I sleep at his palace, and even perch on his nose. I dance and play there, and even pinch him on the cheek." He scorned the Ant, who lived with the Bourgeois. But the Ant's reply expressed her sense of repose. "Aren't you afraid for your life?" she said. *Many people frivolously brag of being happy, and put everybody else down. But neither the beautiful nor the good will be found, if not in something reliable.*

XIII.   La Laitiere/The Milkmaid
         "Castles in Spain" (Dream Castles)

Pérette thought she'd sell her pot of milk, and have a fortune. With pleasurable thoughts she jumped and danced, slipped, and lost all the milk. *The universe is filled with dream castles.*

XIV.   Le Blé, les Moutons, les Loups, et les Hommes/The Wheat, the Sheep, the
       Wolves, and Man
       "Nothing in Excess"

The wheat was uselessly overgrown — too thick, and tufted. The Sheep were brought in to
trim it, but they ruined it by overgrazing. So, to punish them, the Wolves were told to exer-
cise some vengeance on them, but not to eat them all. Now the Wolves did eat them all. So
man was brought in to depopulate the Wolves, because moderation is unknown amongst
men. *"Flee from excess" is the maxim, but people preach it and never take it to themselves.*

XV.   Le Serpent, et la Lime/The Snake and the File
       "Envy"

It is said that at the Watchmaker's, a Snake was looking for something to eat, and could
only find a file made of steel. As he was thinking of chewing it, the file began to sing, "You
are taking on something too hard. Rather than take only a tiny bit of food from me, you
will only break your teeth. I only fear the teeth of time." *Such is virtue. She scarcely fears
envy or wrongdoing. And all the arrows thrown at her never hurt her.*

XVI.   Les Loups, et les Brebis/The Wolves and the Sheep
       "False Peace"

"Let's make an alliance," said the perfidious Wolves to the Sheep. "For collateral we'll take
your Dogs, and keep them well. Our collateral will be the young She-Wolves from our
side." They made the exchange — the Dogs living in the forest, and the young She-Wolves
living with the Sheep. Now weeds take very little time to grow, so the small Wolves soon
grew large, becoming the masters, and butchering the Lambs. *Peace is good, but not with
people of little faith.*

XVII. Les Pigeons, et le Milan/The Pigeons and the Kite
       "False Peace"

Silly is he who trusts his enemy. The light wings of the Pigeons fooled the Kite, so that he
could only catch two or three of them in five or six months. So the enemy (the Kite) had a
ruse, and by beautiful discourse was able to deceive the Pigeons. "Let us have no more war.
I will be yours for protection." The Pigeons responded, "Oh! So much love and goodness,
your Majesty — you may inherit the empire." They made him their despot. You can judge
for yourself what havoc this made. All the Pigeons felt the results of his appetite. *Beware,
my listeners.*

XVIII. Le Fou qui vend la Sagesse/The Fool who sells Wisdom
       "Have no business with Fools"

A certain Fool was selling wisdom — or so he said. Everyone ran to buy it, just as they run
to charlatans. This charlatan made a thousand faces, and gave everyone a couple of slaps,
and a long string (in ancient measurement) for lots of money. If someone got angry, he'd
laugh and make fun of them, saying, "You have what you came for — go figure it out."
What sense did this make? Good sense, you may believe, as the cleverest would say, "Keep
away from this scoundrel, or you'll lose money and honor. *The length of the string he sells
shows us how far to stay away. That is his wisdom.*"

XIX.   L'Aigle, et le Hibou/The Eagle and the Owl
       "Blind Love"

All fathers are crazy about their offspring, even if they are as ugly as a Werewolf. Hear
how the father Owl made a verbal portrait. "Of all birds, mine create the most envy — cute,
well-built, beautiful, graceful, and original." He made this portrayal to the Eagle, so that
when he encountered the little ones he would be lenient. But the Eagle was in the fields one
evening, and found a bunch of grimacing monsters, ugly ones. "I know very well that they
must be the race of my friend the Owl, but these don't look like he said. Should I spare
them? No, truly no." So when Mr. Owl came back and found the carnage, he despaired,

with sadness and rage. The air resounded with his hou-hous. But nobody felt sorry for him. and that which the Eagle had said to the Owl was put in the *Mercure* [*de France*] and told on the Pont-Neuf. [The Pont-Neuf was a bridge over the Seine, where vaudevilles were sung.]

VOLUME SIX

I.   Les Grenouilles qui demandent un Roi/The Frogs who wanted a King
       "The Love of Change"

The Frogs were tired of being a democracy, and clamored so much that they were given a monarchy. "We want a King," they said, "who will keep us under the law." The first one given to them was a plow handle. When he fell from the sky he made so much noise that he scared everyone away, but soon he was quiet and never said or did anything. In his place they put another, who was terrible, and crunched on Frogs. Then they wanted another King, but had to be content with what they had, as a worse one could come along.

II.   Le Rheteur, et le Roi/The Rhetorical Orator, and the King
       "The Charlatans"

A rhetorical orator said, "Bring me an Ass, and I'll make a Doctor out of him." The prince, who had a Jerusalem Donkey, said, "Come and undertake your work. How much time would it take to train him?" "Oh, only about ten years," said the speaker, "but it will take a considerable amount of money." The King had plenty of that. "There will be a clause, that We will hang the teacher if he goes back on his promise." All was agreed. Everyone thought that all would be lost (for the teacher). But in order to be hanged, he knew that he had ten years, and he knew that before that time would come to pass, either the Ass, the King, or himself would die. Not foolish! *Sometimes the Prince himself is led by the nose.*

III.   Le Cheval, et l'Ane /The Horse and the Ass
       "Inhumanity"

A horse was having a grand time on the trip. He had only his harness, as the baggage was carried by an overburdened Ass, who said, "I can't go on. Take one of these two baskets which are my load. It would only be a plaything for your Lordship. If you don't, it will be all over for me." The Horse responded with laughter, but his comrade did die. He would have done better to listen to his plea, for they now took the whole load from the Ass and put it on the Horse — including the skin of the Ass. So, just like human beings, the Horse laughed at other's pains. And far from helping, one piles on oppression upon oppression. *Every day the little ones succumb, but their burdens fall upon those who make fun of them.*

IV.   Le Loup, la Mere et l'Enfant/The Wolf, the Mother and the Child
       "Foolish Expectation"

The mother's child was crying, so in order to quiet him she said to him, "I'm going to go away! I swear I'll leave you to the Wolf!" Just by chance the Wolf heard this. The gluttonous beast waited for his chance, thinking that after the mother had given this threat, he was owed this pleasure. But he didn't know that the threat was just a face she made in anger. So the wolf at the door was perceived, and well received. The people killed him.

V.   Le Loup et la Cicogne/The Wolf and the Stork [Cicogne-Cigogne]
       "The Ingratitude of Great People"

Eating until he was satiated, one of the gluttonous Wolves had a bone of lamb stuck in his throat. A Stork came by, and got to the task — getting the bone out of his throat. "What will you give me for such a service," he said. The Wolf replied, "The payment is your life — that I haven't killed you. Isn't that enough? Your neck is without damage, and had just come out of my muzzle unscathed. It seems to me that you are wrong if you expect any more from a great person."

VI.　Le Torrent, et la Rivière/The Torrent and the River
　　　"Cunning"

A Torrent flowed down the mountain with a great noise, being vomited from the innards of the mountain. There was a certain merchant who was fleeing a robber. He encountered this barrier (the Torrent) and crossed it happily, as the waves were noisy, but without depth. The thief also passed. The man, therefore, was still in a hurry. He next found a river which was quiet, like a basin. The man believed (wrongly) that this channel was without danger also. But it had a deep abyss which he could not cross. He fought, but drowned. *So let us beware of underhanded people — they are nasty but silent.*

VII.　Le Levraut, et la Tortue/The Tortoise and the Hare
　　　"Make Haste Slowly"

He who leaves from an appointed mark runs and gallops in vain. The Tortoise renders himself to the goal, rather than the Hare. They made a wager. "Let's go," said the one, "I only need two instants." The other set out first, and lost no time. One could see the runner almost at the end of the road, but he got caught in a trap, so all his running was to no effect. The beast which one had said would lose got the honor and the profit.

VIII.　Le Trésor et les deux Hommes/The Treasure and the Two Men
　　　"Avarice"

It is a tragedy about which I'm going to sing, or maybe a comedy — your choice. A beggar wanted an end to his poverty. So he got a plan to strangle himself, and went to the height of a barn to drive in a nail to put a noose on. But while doing so, he found a treasure in the wall, and took it, leaving the cord with which he planned to hang himself had not the treasure come along. But the Proprieter, who heard this, came running. He saw his money gone, and only the cord remaining. "I'll save some money," he said. "This cord was left for me, and I'll hang myself with it."

IX.　Le Coq, et la Perle/The Rooster and the Pearl
　　　"Trade Given"

"I would like to find someone who would trade with me," said a Rooster. "It's a fine pearl I found, but I'd rather some grain for my kitchen." *Important works, paintings, manuscripts to ignorant eyes are always a vile prize. What good is an antique medal in the home of some village fool? The fool, whatever it is worth, would not sell it for its value.*

X.　L'Hirondelle, et le Rossignol/The Swallow and the Nightingale
　　　"No Beautiful Prisons"

The Swallow went into the woods to see the Nightingale, and found her sister there, singing re mi fa sol la. "What are you doing here?" she said. "Don't you know that what charms the animals could also attract some rustic character who would hear it and be envious of your song? Come to the King's palace. You'll have a golden house, happiness, and all your needs met." "But add to that," replied the singer, "a beautiful and sad captivity. Where would I be without liberty?" *Any slavery is detestable.*

XI.　Le Loup, et le Chien/The Wolf and the Dog
　　　"Liberty"

Nothing can compensate for liberty. The heart prizes it above wealth and beauty. "No," said the Wolf to the fattened Dog. "Your situation is not desirable. In vain you think you are fortunate. If I am poor, at least I am not in chains."

XII.　L'Ecrevisse, et la Chenille/The Crayfish and the Caterpillar
　　　"Example"

The Caterpillar said to the Crayfish, "You reprimand your daughter without any right, for a child in a family can only do what it sees. It is the example that directs us; without it you teach uselessly. It is in vain that one corrects others when he himself is perverse. Will one go straight, when the example is set by one who walks backwards?"

XIII.   La Grenouille, et le Rat/The Frog and the Rat
         "Treachery"

On a green river, a Rat was taking some air, when along came the Queen of the swamp — the Frog. "Oh! I'm so glad to see you, " said the hypocrite gently. "Come, come to my place, where the home is beautiful, and the baths agreeable." But the Rat said that without any help, he wouldn't know how to swim. The Frog said, "We can remedy that easily. I'll make you a little boat, and attach it to my foot so you can follow along." But the Frog dove to the bottom, to make a juicy tidbit of the Rat. The Rat cried out, but the Frog pulled him into the depths. Then a Kite came along, and lifted them all up by the cord. *Treachery often harms its own author.*

XIV.   L'Alouette, l'Autour, et l'Oiseleur/The Lark, the Goshawk, and the Fowler
         "No mercy to one who gives none"

With difficulty and pain, the Lark found herself trapped in a net. A Goshawk saw the poor thing, and descended upon her like a flash. She begged in vain, but he started to eat her. While she was crying, the Fowler came along, and grabbed the gluttonous Goshawk. So just as the Lark cried out for mercy, it happened to him also. *You who do not give mercy: Should one accord it to you?*

XV.   Le Chapon, et le Faucon/The Capon and the Falcon
         "Defiance"

A Capon that one wished to take as a bit of food for a feast, didn't want to give himself up, and took sudden flight towards the fields. All the people in the kitchen said, "Come, come, little one." But he fled. A Falcon intercepted him, and said, "You poor thing, no one can teach you anything. I'm different — I sit on the wrist of the Master when he wishes. I fly to him when he wishes. Don't you want to go too?" The other one replied, "Tell me another one! Would you go if when they called you they were armed with a big knife?"

XVI.   Les Bâtons flottans/Floating Sticks
         "Appearance"

Seeing some sticks floating on the water, from afar one would say it's a big ship, then only a small ship, then people would laugh — seeing that it is just a bundle of sticks. There are many people in this world who from afar appear really great, but then close up are a frivolous object, a worm that shines, a piece of straw — worthy of disdain.

XVII.   Le Dauphin, et la Guenon/The Dolphin, and the Ape
         "Foolish Liar"

This is about a liar. I have my story from a very good source, who tells us that a ship was sinking, and all the sailors would have perished if a Dolphin had not taken them on his back. But an Ape straddled the Dolphin's back, who at first took the Ape for a Man. But in wondering about this, he asked him questions, and got him to reveal his game. "Are you from Athen, or Argos?" And the Ape replied, "I am one of the wise ones from Athens, and Pyrée is my friend." (Pyrée is a port at Athens.) The Dolphin realized his error, saying, "I thought I was carrying a great musician, but it's only an Ape. I do not wish such an ugly load. Ugly liar, into the water with you." And he plunged into the water, the Ape falling to the bottom.

XVIII.   Le Singe et le Chat/The Monkey and the Cat
         "The Rogues"

Bertrand Monkey and Raton the Cat were famous rogues, and they lived together in peace. The first of these thieves saw some chestnuts in the fire. "How can we get them?" he asked.

So the Cat spread the cinders and coals apart to get the chestnuts. But how can one play with fire without getting burned? The Cat did suffer, and sometimes cried out with a piercing scream. At this noise the cook's boy came running with a stick. *All the stealing was done for the Monkey, but it was the Cat which paid the tab.*

XIX.   Le Berger, et le Troupeau/The Shepherd and the Flock
       "False Brave Ones"

"I have lost," said Coridon the Shepherd, "a sheep every day. And here I am without any help against the glutton. The Bull Sheep don't spare any energy in the combats against each other, but they won't even take a step against the Wolf." A few moments later one cried out, "There he is!" It was only a shadow which sent them running. If you had a hundred squadrons of cowardly men, the mere name of the enemy would make all your fanfares in vain. Your Giants would be turned into Ants.

XX.   Le Loup, et le Cheval/The Wolf and the Horse
       "The Cheat who was duped"

A Wolf saw a Horse grazing in the corner of a pasture. He seemed a little sick, but strong nevertheless — and a little naive. The Wolf decided on a really good trick. He arrived, announcing himself as a Doctor and bragging about his knowledge — recounting all sorts of stories about how he cured horses with his magical book. And he flattered himself with his great memory. The Horse (being a little suspicious,) said, "Look, it's only a little wound I have, and it's on my back foot." What did the foolish one do? The Wolf approached his eyes to the back hoof. The Horse took his time, then let go with a blow — hitting him in the mouth, and making paste of his teeth. *Many people lose by their own machinations.*

XXI.   Le Rossignol, et l'Autour/The Nightingale and the Goshawk
       "The Hungry Stomach has no Ears"

Philomèle, the great singer, was in the talons of the Goshawk, and said to him in vain, "My plumage is the love of Kings themselves." But the Goshawk replied, "That's their business. As for me, it is hardly that you are here for me to hear you sing. Your wonderful listeners, without doubt, have dined at ease. You may think that I listen to you, but I have not had lunch. An empty stomach does not have ears to hear a song. One does not dine on sound." Thus said, he ate her. *Eloquence will not save you from barbarous ones.*

XXII.   Le Cigne, et le Cuisinier/The Swan and the Cook
       "Soft Words"

In a menagerie a Swan lived with a Goose. The Swan sang songs to the Master. The second one was only there to be served up in a meal. But by error, the officer, who had too much to drink, grabbed the Swan instead of the Goose. The singer was lost — he was going to put her into the soup. Happily the singer complained, and the tone of his chirping confused the man. "Go," he said, "and pardon me for having made a mistake. I want the Goose, whose cries are unpleasant." *Learn, and remember, that it won't harm you to speak softly.*

XXIII. Le Loup, et les Bergers/The Wolf and the Shepherds
       "Poor Example"

A Wolf, as it is told, had one day some regrets and shame for his excesses and cruelty. "On all the earth I am hated, and everyone is arming up against me. Where does all this rage come from, with which they pursue me? Is it from some Lamb that I ate, or a Dog? Is it worth all this for me to be the butt of such arrows? Let's prevent violence and hatred. I'll chomp and graze in fallow fields." But as he was talking he saw near him, just by chance, a Lamb being roasted on a spit in an orchard. "What!" said he. "I am afraid to do what those Men are doing? I will fall like Hercules upon the Calves and the Sheep. It would be ridiculous to reduce myself to eating thistles. My scruples were folly. Back to my former life!"

APPENDIX

The Review from the *Mercure de France* in Facsimile

Il faut donc pour cette Fête,
Aux Dieux, fans autre façon,
Prefenter notre Requête,
Les priant d'y mettre, *Bon*.
Mais *Bon* depuis le quinziéme
De Janvier jufqu'au trentiéme.
On en doit tout efperer;
C'eft pour eux fi peu de chofe,
Qu'ils daigneront l'accorder;
C'eft fur quoi je me repofe.

Il paroît un Ouvrage qui a pour titre, *Poëfies Spirituelles & Morales fur les plus beaux Airs de la Mufique Françoife & Italienne*. Premier Recueil, prix 6. livres en blanc. *A Paris chez Guillaume Defprez, Libraire, ruë S. Jacques, à S. Profper, Ph. N. Lottin, à la Verité, & Guichard, Marchand Papetier de la Mufique du Roi, ruë de l'Arbre-fec, derriere S. Germain l'Auxerrois*; ç'eft un in 4. gravé, grand papier.

On s'eft propofé dans ce Recueil de donner un effai de l'ufage chrétien & raifonnable qu'on peut faire de la Mufique. Il commence par un Cantique affez étendu fur les grandeurs de Dieu, dont la Mufique eft du celebre M. *Defmarets*, & la Poëfie d'un grand Maître. On en peut juger par les deux premieres Strophes que nous allons rapporter.   Loin

Loin d'ici, profanes Mortels,
Vous dont la main impie a dreffé des Autels,
A des Dieux impuiffans que le crime a fait naître,
Qu'aux accens de ma voix tout tremble en l'Univers,
Cieux, Enfers, Terre, Mers, c'eft votre augufte Maître,
Que je vais chanter dans mes Vers.

Il eft, & par lui feul tout Etre a pris naiffance
Le néant exifte à fa voix:
La Nature & les temps agiffent par fes Loix;
Tout adore en tremblant fa fuprême puiffance.
Invifible & prefent, on le trouve en tous lieux,
Il remplit la Terre & les Cieux;
Par lui tout fe meut, tout refpire;
Sa durée eft l'Eternité,
Et les bornes de fon Empire,
Sont celles de l'immenfité.

On trouve enfuite des Cantiques fur les Myfteres de Notre Seigneur, fur les Vertus & les Vices, & fur les quatre Fins de l'homme. Ce Recueil renferme tous les fujets de pieté qu'on peut defirer. On y trouve auffi d'autres Pieces que l'on peut appeller des *Chanfons Morales*, & qui peuvent fervir dans des occafions où les premieres paroîtroient peut-être trop férieufes.
F iiij

rieuſes. Pour intereſſer par la varieté, on a recueilli près d'une centaine d'Airs ſur tous les differens caracteres de la Muſique. Pluſieurs Muſettes, Airs de Violon, Pieces de Clavecin de M. Couprin, Airs Italiens & pluſieurs doubles dans le gout de M. Lambert.

On eſpere que les perſonnes qui auront de la voix ſeront bien aiſes qu'on leur fourniſſe le moyen d'en faire un uſage utile, quand elles voudront elles-mêmes prendre ce délaſſement, ou qu'elles ne pourront le refuſer à d'autres qui voudront les entendre chanter.

On a ajoûté à ce Recueil grand nombre de Fables choiſies, dans le gout de la Fontaine, ſur les petits Airs & Vaudevilles les plus connus, avec une Baſſe en Muſette, qui pourront ſervir au même uſage que les Chanſons Morales dont on vient de parler, mais qui ſont deſtinées principalement à fournir aux Enfans un amuſement utile & convenable à leur âge: nous en rapporterons deux pour ſervir d'exemple.

L'UTILE ET LE BEAU.

Le Cerf ſe mirant dans l'eau. Sur l'Air: *Je fais ſouvent raiſonner ma Muſette*, & ſur *les Folies d'Eſpagne*.

Dans le Criſtal d'une claire Fontaine,
Un jeune Cerf ſe miroit autrefois;

Il ne voyoit ſes jambes qu'avec peine,
Charmé de voir la beauté de ſon Bois.

Soudain du Cor entendant le murmure,
Prompt & leger, il fuit dans les Forêts;
Mais arrêté par ſa belle ramure,
En expirant il pouſſe ces regrets.

Le beau nous plaît & le bien nous ennuye,
L'un ſert toûjours, l'autre eſt ſouvent fatal,
Je mépriſois ce qui ſauvoit ma vie,
J'aimois, helas! ce qui fait tout mon mal.

LA PEUR.

Les Oreilles du Lievre. Sur l'Air: *C'eſt une Bouteille qui n'eut jamais ſa pareille.*

De ſa corne un inconnu,
Au Lion fit quelque peine.
Lion dit, que tout Cornu,
Soit chaſſé de mon Domaine.
Depuis le Taureau juſqu'au Chevreau,
Tout s'en va chercher pays nouveau.
Le bruit en vent au Lievre,
Qui de crainte en a la fievre.

Ah! dit-il, je ſuis banni,
J'ai deux cornes bien pareilles.

Et Oa

On lui dit en vain, nenni,
Ce ne font que des oreilles.
Il répond toûjours, détrompez-vous;
Au gré des malins & des jaloux,
Oreilles feront cornes,
Voire cornes de Licornes.

🜲

C'eſt ainſi, quand on a peur,
Que tout ſe metamorphoſe;
Un Buiſſon eſt un Voleur,
Un Phantôme, ou pire choſe,
Mais on ſçait de même qu'à la Cour,
Un flateur fait prendre chaque jour,
Les Merles pour Corneilles,
Et pour cornes les Oreilles.

On promet de donner inceſſamment un ſecond Recueil de Fables dans le même goût, & de les réünir enſuite toutes enſemble dans un petit volume avec les airs notez, afin qu'en puiſſe s'en ſervir plus commodément.

Sans vouloir prévenir le jugement du Public, ce Recueil nous paroît être un excellent mélange de l'utile & de l'agréable. Une pieté tendre & ſolide, la nobleſſe des penſées & des ſentimens, le naïf des Fables, le choix & la varieté des Airs parfaitement aſſortis aux paroles

paroles; tout invite également ceux qui ne cherchent pas dans la Muſique un vain amuſement ou un plaiſir dangereux. On n'a rien épargné pour leur plaire : la beauté de la Gravure & du papier, & la modicité du prix font aſſez voir que ceux qui ont entrepris ce Recueil, n'ont eu en vüe que l'avantage du Public.

On écrit d'Amſterdam, que M. *Bourguet* a donné chez François l'Honoré des Lettres Philoſophiques ſur la formation des Sels & Cryſtaux, & ſur la generation & le mecaniſme organique des Plantes & des Animaux, à l'occaſion de la pierre Belemnite & de la pierre Lenticulaire, avec un Mémoire ſur la Théorie de la terre. Ces quatre Lettres ſont adreſſées à M. J. Scheuchzer.

M. *Durand*, au College de Gresham à Londres, Membre de la Societé Royale, a compoſé & diſtribué l'*Hiſtoire de l'Or & de l'Argent*, extraite de *Pline* le Naturaliſte, L. 33. avec un ſuplément à l'hiſtoire de l'Or. *Vol. in-folio.*

Le Sieur Chevillard, Généalogiſte du Roy, Chronologiſte & Hiſtoriographe de France, (qualitez qui lui furent accordées par Lettres du Grand Sceau du 19.
F vj Fevrier

Index to the Edition

The following is an alphabetical listing of the *Fables*. After the title of each fable there appears the page on which that fable will be found in this edition, then the volume number and fable number, then the number of the air to which the fable is set. (With the exception of the pagination of this edition, the volume, fable, and air numbering in the original has been retained.) When the fable is only to be sung to an air which appears in a different volume than the text, the words "to be sung to" are followed by the volume number, air, and page on which the air may be found in this edition. When the fable appears in the original with its air, but may also be sung to another air, the words "May also be sung to" appear, with the appropriate volume, air, and page number.

Le Renard, et le Buste p. 75, Vol. II, Fable X, Air VI.

Le Renard, et le Chat p. 82, Vol. II, Fable XX, to be sung to Vol. I, Air 1, p.43.

Le Renard, et le Lion p. 106, Vol. IV, Fable IX, Air V.

Le Renard, & le Loup p. 54, Vol. I, Fable XI, Air VIII.

Le Renard, & les Raisins p. 58, Vol. I, Fable XIX, Air XIII.

Le Rheteur, et le Roi p. 138, Vol. VI, Fable II, Air II.

Le Rossignol, et l'Autour p. 155, Vol. VI, Fable XXI, to be sung to Vol. I, Air XIII, p. 58.

Le Satire, et son Hôte p. 88, Vol. III, Fable IV, Air III.

Le Savetier enrichi p. 94, Vol. III, Fable X, Air VII.

Le Serpent, et la Lime p.132, Vol. V, Fable XV, Air VII.

Le Serpent, et le Villageois p. 117, Vol. IV, Fable XXII to be sung to Vol. I, Air II, p. 44

Le Singe adopté p. 87, Vol. III, Fable III, Air II.

Le Singe et le Chat p. 153, Vol. VI, Fable XVII, Air X.

Le Singe, et le Leopard p. 93, Vol. III, Fable IX, Air VI.

Le Souriceau, et sa Mere p. 122, Vol. V, Fable V to be sing to Vol. II, Air IV, p. 71.

Le Statuaire p. 76, Vol. II, Fable XI, Air VII.

La Torrent, et la Rivière p. 142, Vol. VI, Fable VI, Air IV.

La Tortue, et l'Aigle p. 127, Vol. V, Fable IX, Air V.

La Tortue, et les Deux Canards p. 79, Vol. II, Fable XVI, Air X.

Le Trésor, et les deux Hommes p. 144, Vol. VI, Fable VIII, Air V. May also be sung to Vol. I, Air VI, p. 50.

Le Vieillard, et ses Enfans p. 119, Vol. V, Fable I, Air I.

La Vieille, et les deux Servantes p. 91, Vol. III, Fable VII, Air V.